Sanctuaries
of Childhood

Also by Shea Darian:

Books

Seven Times the Sun:
Guiding Your Child Through the Rhythms of the Day

Grandpa's Garden

CD's

Celtic Quest/Avalon a cappella

Sanctuaries
of Childhood

Nurturing a Child's Spiritual Life

Shea Darian

Gilead Press

Gilead Press
P.O. Box 727
Marshall, WI   53559

To order: call or fax (608) 655-1023
or e-mail: gilead@jvlnet.com

Library of Congress Cataloging-in-Publication Data
Darian, Shea, 1959-
    Sanctuaries of childhood: nurturing a child's spiritual life
        p.   cm.
    Includes bibliographical references and indexes.
    ISBN 0-9675713-1-6
    1. Parent and child-Miscellanea. 2. Family-Religious Life-Miscellanea. I. Title.
    II. Title: Sanctuaries of childhood
    HQ755.8.D375   2001   00-192146
    649.1 — dc21   CIP

*Grateful acknowledgment is made for permission to reprint the following copyrighted
material. Every effort has been made to trace ownership of all copyrighted material. If
any omission has been made, please bring this to the attention of the publisher so that
proper acknowledgment may be given in future editions.*

Quotation from the article, "The Hidden Meaning in Fairy Tales," by Margret Meyerkort,
from Lifeways: Working with Family Questions, reprinted 2000, Hawthorn Press, Stroud,
Gloucestershire GL5 1BJ, Great Britain. (www.hawthornpress.com)

Quotation from *Emily* by Michael Bedard. Copyright 1992 by Michael Bedard, reprinted
by permission of Random House Children's Books, a division of Random House, Inc.

To my mother, Demetra Anne Woodyard,
who gave me the provisions to make the journey;

and to my father, Charles Bagbey,
who inspired me with the courage
to find my own way.

Thank you to. . .

Those who were willing to read and comment on the
manuscript as it took form:

Sally Celenza, Dan Corwin-Renner,
Tammy Corwin-Renner, Rebecca Danica,
Andrew Darian, Julie Howard, Kate Jolin,
Dana Larson, and Mary Truman

My sister, Rebecca Danica, and my friend, Polly Hamann,
for being sources of constant encouragement

My friend, Lisa Bagbey,
for her exceptional proofing skills

My children, Morgan and Willa,
who are two of my greatest teachers

And my spouse, Andrew Darian,
who is forever a sanctuary for my soul

Table of Contents

A Note to the Reader

Sanctuaries of Childhood: Nurturing a Child's Spiritual Life is an entreaty to parents, grandparents, and caregivers. An entreaty to bridge the chasm too often created in our children's lives, which separates them from their spiritual selves. An entreaty to fill the spiritual void our children experience from living in a fast-paced electronic age, in which they are showered with *information* but sorely lacking *inspiration*.

This book is intended for parents, grandparents, and caregivers of ALL faiths. Whether you are a member of a traditional religious faith, a newly formed spiritual community, or feel disconnected from any organized religion, *Sanctuaries of Childhood* welcomes you to consider how childhood, at its best, is a spiritual playground. A playground where the sacred is constantly at our fingertips.

Whatever your religious background may be, please consider the contents of this book as a (hopefully inspiring) conversation. Given your unique spiritual journey, some sections of *Sanctuaries of Childhood* may be more helpful than others. Allow these ideas to be a catalyst for discovering how you and your family can best strengthen your own faith journey.

Throughout the book, I often use the words "God" and "Divine Spirit" interchangeably. Whatever word is most meaningful for you, in naming a "Higher Power," please feel free to insert it in your reading. Also, feel free to change any words in the songs and verses offered throughout this book to make them more meaningful for you and the children in your life.

I believe we have no greater work than to encourage children to cultivate lives of genuine spiritual devotion. The future of our planet and the spiritual well-being of our children (and our children's children) depend upon it. In our fast-moving society, striving toward a more balanced, harmonious family life requires a great deal of us — body, heart, mind, soul, and spirit. Please remember to take this journey one step at a time. Each sanctuary we build with the children in our lives requires effort and intentionality. The spiritual renewal and joy we experience as a result, is the grace by which we continue our journey one step at a time. One faithful step at a time.

Sanctuaries of Childhood

Preface ∽ A Sacred Trust

I do not know how you appeared in my womb;
it was not I who endowed you with breath and life,
I had not the shaping of your every part.

> ~ Mother of Seven Sons
> (from the Hebrew Scriptures)

When I was pregnant with my first child and felt the flutterings of her life inside me, and when I held her for the first time in my arms and looked into her newborn eyes, there was no doubt in me that she was more divine than earthly. I sensed that she had come to me straight from the arms of God. And I knew that in receiving her life into my care, I was agreeing to uphold a sacred trust, not only to feed, clothe, and protect her physical body, but to nourish and protect her soul-life as well.

As a society, we give little time or energy to the nourishment of our children's souls, and thus, the deepening of their spiritual relationships. Our busy lives make it difficult. In recent years, I have spoken with many parents and grandparents who tell me it is not only time they are lacking. They tell me of their feelings of inadequacy to guide their children spiritually. They say that they often fumble in knowing where to begin, or get lost along the way as a child moves on to a new stage of development. Some parents enroll their children in a religious education program, hoping a child can receive at church or synagogue what the parent feels inadequate to provide. Thus, many children experience a void, as their most significant spiritual teachers imagine themselves to be ill-qualified for the task.

I believe that even more significant than sharing our chosen religion with our children, as important as this may be for their spiritual growth, is providing a home and family life that allows a child to experience and recognize the divine qualities of goodness, beauty, and wisdom. Sharing any form of "religion" with a child that fails to do so, is like asking a child to make a journey on a bicycle with no handle bars or tires. In traveling to the destination, the bicycle will be of little use to the child and easily discarded.

My hope in guiding children toward lives of spiritual devotion is to bathe them with the experience of *genuine* religion, for "religion" means literally *to reconnect with the Divine*. It means hollowing out space in our everyday lives to make room for the sacred. It means being awake to our living relationships with the world of the Spirit. It means opening our ears to the Divine voices within and around us.

My greatest vision is a world transformed by the uncovering of *true* religion in our homes and our larger faith communities. For, if children receive the opportunity to take into their very souls the goodness, beauty, and wisdom of creation, they are enabled to become adults who serve creation out of the goodness, beauty, and wisdom of their souls.

When we invite the Divine Spirit to commune with us in our most intimate relationships, we create a vessel out of which that Spirit may live, may move through our society and through our entire global village. As parents and caregivers who are committed to nurturing the souls of our children, we are helping to change the world for good, one child, one family at a time.

∞ The Sanctuaries

Know you what it is to be a child? It is to be something very different from the (adult) of today. It is
to have a spirit yet streaming from the waters of bap-
tism; it is to believe in love, to believe in loveliness,
to believe in belief; it is to be so little that the elves
can reach to whisper in your ear; it is to turn pump-
kins into coaches, and mice into horses, lowness into
loftiness, and nothing into everything, for each child
has its fairy godmother in its soul.

- Francis Thompson

The sanctuaries of childhood are numerous and open to all. They are not built upon divisions of sect, race, or nation. The sanctuaries of childhood are universal. They are the everyday, sacred spaces in which a child experiences the interwoven connection between the physical and spiritual — through the wonder of nature, the magic of song, the joy of helping another, the comfort of being held in a loving, supportive family circle. . . through poetry and prayer. Each of these sanctuaries provides a haven in which a child's soul may be nurtured and their spiritual relationships and understanding deepened.

We live in a society that makes it ever more difficult for children to find access to these sanctuaries on a daily basis. More consistently, entrance to such sacred spaces is being barred by the obstacles of busy schedules, our overuse of television and electronic media, and a lack of understanding for a child's genuine spiritual needs. Parents and caregivers can help to unbolt the doors of these sanctuaries, and make it possible for children to experience divine comfort and inspiration.

As we make room in our lives for children to share with us the sacred qualities of childhood, no doubt young and old will find that within the sanctuaries of childhood, we serve one another as rabbis, ministers, and spiritual teachers. So let us open wide the doors. Let us remember what it is to be a child. . .

1 ∞ A Sacred Circle

The Sanctuary of Family Life

Common as light is love,
And its familiar voice
wearies not ever. . .

- Percy Bysshe Shelley

Entering the Sanctuary of Family Life

Some folks say we choose our families before we are conceived, while we are still on the other side of that threshold between worlds. For me, this picture is a great solace. I delight in thinking of my children as souls, musing through the misty veil at my foibles and shortcomings. It heartens me many a day to think they would know me and still want me as their mother.

Perhaps this is the sacred key to our time here on earth, to be so humbled by another's love that we realize perfection pales in comparison to sincerity. As we embrace the mystery of love, we see that it contains not an absence of error, but the presence of grace. It contains not the absence of anger or pain, but the presence of forgiveness and healing. Not the absence of disharmony or confusion, but the presence of peace and clarity.

To make a home into a sanctuary, we must be willing to make room in our hearts for one another's limitations, as well as our gifts. For it is here in this sacred space of the home and family, so brimming with life, so full of every emotion available to our hearts, that we learn what it means to love within all the nuances of an intimate relationship. We learn to unlock gateway after gateway that would keep us from throwing ourselves unabashedly once again into one another's arms.

I grew up in Iowa, the youngest of four children. One summer when I was seven, my older sister, Rebecca, and I were sent to my grandmother's house in Little Rock, Arkansas, for a three-week stay. Within a few days, my sister and I were eager to return home, for my grandmother (bless her soul) didn't particularly like or understand children. Our time together proved to be difficult for all of us. My sister and I were relieved to return home and vowed never to be sent away from home by ourselves again. Yet, for me, the entire episode was worth the memory of our return.

As we dragged our bags into the house and up the stairs to our bedrooms, we were halted midway up the staircase by the sound of our then thirteen-year-old brother, Roger, bursting through the front door. (We learned later that he had "caught wind" a few blocks away that his sisters had returned home.)

Roger bounced up the stairs two at a time, flung his arms around us, and nearly carried us the rest of the way to the second floor, all the while babbling loud, ecstatic exclamations of his love for us and his joy in our return. My seven-year-old heart swelled with pride at this unabashed display of affection. To be so honored by a thirteen-year-old brother, who could be as much of a bother and a tease as any brother ever could, was a highlight of my summer.

Whenever I looked at my brother after that as we were growing up, I could see his capacity for devotion and affection, every bit as clearly as I could see his capacity for orneriness. Even now, the memory of this homecoming and the deepening intimacy it cultivated, inspires me to give such uninhibited honor to those I hold dear, to become, at times, a "babbling fool" in the name of love.

When my partner, Andrew, and I celebrated our 10th wedding anniversary, it felt like a relational milestone. A decade of deepening affection for the one person we know better than any other, save ourselves. For days during and after our celebration, I walked around with a tender feeling in my heart. Each time I looked at Andrew or either of our children, I was reminded of the fragile miracle that each of these relationships holds for me. And I smiled with the memory of all the years, before Andrew and I met, that I told myself I would never marry and "have a family" — for fear of the freedom it would cost me.

I see now that without my family, there is a kind of freedom I may never have encountered in my lifetime. For as my family learns to create a sanctuary of healthy relationships, we experience the freedom of being who we are, who we are becoming, in an atmosphere of respect and love. Oh, there is no denying that we must wrestle with one another's boundaries, expectations, wants, and desires. At times, this requires a good bit of personal sacrifice. Yet, there is also no denying that within this sanctuary of family life, built on the substance of our affection, that we also find freedom — the kind of freedom one may only encounter in the abode where love resides.

Ministering to Children
in the Sanctuary of Family Life

When I was in seminary, I had a friend whose father was a minister. Both of my friend's parents were well-known in their church denomination for the work they had done in the areas of social justice and world peace. Having a strong interest in social transformation, I often thought how fortunate my friend was to have two such committed, influential parents.

Then, one evening, my friend confided in me that he had been utterly lonely growing up. He said his parents were always flitting this way or that, working for one cause or another. My friend told me that what he wanted more than anything, as a child, was for his parents to show him that they cared as much for *him* as they cared for the homeless person on the street or the child in South Africa.

Recalling my friend's story in the first few years of parenting, was a great motivator, for even after I had become one, I had difficulty envisioning myself as a "homemaker." Indeed, the title frightened me. Conjured up images of me watching an entire cycle of precious years fade away into mountains of dirty dishes, a chorus of mouths to feed, skinned knees to bandage, diapers to change. When I decided to stay home with two young children and become what some call a "full-time parent," I feared I was forsaking my opportunity to "really make a difference" in the world. While my graduate school buddies were pursuing interesting, challenging careers, I was sweeping floors, wiping noses, singing children to sleep.

Yet, as I committed myself to the challenge, and as the days, weeks and months cycled on, I became ever more convinced that parenting healthy children, more than any work I knew, had the potential to change the world for good in ways little else could. Rather than bemoan the fact that my work was not having an immediate impact on the larger communities of my life, I began to look at my passions for social transformation and world peace in the context of my own family.

I began to see that creating a healthy family, in which members develop the ability for mutual respect and caring, is a prerequisite for a more peaceful world. For, it is the family that creates the social fabric of our culture, as Mahatma Gandhi so poignantly illustrated, when he said:

> If we are to teach real peace in this world. . . we shall have to begin with children; and if they will grow up in their own innocence, we won't have to struggle; we won't have to pass fruitless, idle resolutions, but we shall go from love to love and peace to peace, until at last all the corners of the world are covered with that peace and love for which, consciously or unconsciously, the whole world is hungering.

Sweeping floors, wiping noses, singing children to sleep. . . such is the work of the peacemakers. Blessed be the peacemakers.

Seeking Wisdom in Family Life

Seeds of Freedom

I am learning to listen to my children, listen beyond their verbal pleas, their fleeting whims and wants of any given moment. I am learning to understand the language of my children's deeper yearnings. Learning to listen to them with my very soul.

I know many parents, including myself, who are striving to raise children to become the unique individual each was created to become. We talk of fostering a home environment that will encourage children to think and act freely, so they may boldly help to build a more equitable, loving, and peaceful society.

In response to the overly strict "discipline" of past generations, many parents have begun to allow their children "freedoms" which were unthinkable 30 or 40 years ago. Some children, even very young ones, are not only making decisions about what breakfast cereal to eat or what clothes to wear to school, but also what school they will attend, in which divorced parent's house they will reside from one day to the next, what time they will go to bed each night.

We live in a society in which permissiveness is frequently displacing the intentional care required for children to become the "free individuals" we so desire them to become — individuals with whom others will actually want to relate. Through our permissiveness, we are making it difficult for children to learn to identify and respect their own needs and the needs of others.

Recently, I attended a breakfast gathering where a mother and father (intelligent, committed parents) allowed their 3 1/2-year-old to scream through the entire meal, without removing her from the room.

Needless to say, the enjoyment of the occasion for all of us was made difficult. The child went her way after the meal laughing and playing, while the rest of us struggled with indigestion. Young children need not have such power over us. Failing to respond appropriately and consistently to a child's calls for guidance, forces the child to develop manipulative relationships with us in which they seek our attention any way they can get it.

The boundaries we set for children in their younger years become the substance they use to build boundaries for themselves as they mature. For children to grow into clear-thinking teenagers, they must first experience the guidance of clear-thinking caregivers. From our example, children internalize such qualities as thoughtfulness and decisiveness. The more lovingly and consistently we model these qualities for them, the more apt they are to acquire the tools they will need to meet the joys and challenges of their growing independence in adolescence and adulthood.

As we learn to develop healthy, helpful relationships with our children, let us remember that *discipline begins with ourselves*. It is not a punishment we impose upon our children, but an art of living that we teach them. Discipline and freedom are not opposites. Discipline is the seed by which freedom is planted.

The Daily Round

In our fast-paced society, we have become more and more disconnected with the natural rhythms of the day — which offer a balance of activity and rest, interaction and solitude, work and play. Yet, more and more people, who are attempting to live by spiritual values which promote being in the present and cultivating peace and balance, have rediscovered the joy and meaning we find when we honor these natural rhythms.

Few parenting tools can alleviate more frustrations, conflicts, and misbehavior on the part of children and parents alike than creating a more rhythmic pattern for daily life in the family. In this way, everyone knows generally what to expect, and children and parents can breathe more easily and feel more secure as we make our "daily round." A time for morning prayers, regular mealtimes and rest times, a bedtime story, a daily walk — such simple everyday rituals can be the path to contentment, joy, and peace. As Andrew and I have cultivated greater rhythm in our family over the past several years, we have witnessed our joy, patience, and clarity grow accordingly.

Although consistent daily rhythms are an imperative part of the young child's day, family members of all ages can be deeply nourished by a more rhythmic lifestyle. Of course, as our children mature, our approach and tools for creating family rhythms and rituals will evolve, as well. For further inspiration, you may want to read my previous book, *Seven Times the Sun: Guiding Your Child Through the Rhythms of the Day*, which offers a myriad of resources for creating rhythm in family life.

Visions of Beauty

William Morris once wrote, "Have nothing in your houses that you do not know to be useful, or believe to be beautiful." When we are surrounded by an uncluttered, useful, beautiful environment, our thinking, feelings, and actions become more uncluttered, purposeful, and beautiful as well. This is especially true for young children, who are like sponges, absorbing everything from the world around them. That everything includes news reports we think they aren't listening to and adult conversation that isn't meant for their ears.

Encourage yourself to find one small, or not so small, way each week to make your home a more useful and beautiful place to nurture family. Arrange more bouquets, light more candles, hang more pictures that may truly be called "art." Choose more colors that have a peaceful, inspiring affect on the soul. Allow silence to be your "background music." Put up some new shelves. Collect less junk. Reorganize a room or closet. Make television viewing and computer games the exception rather than the norm. Go on a news fast for a week.

Let us remember that the less clutter we accumulate, the more we can see one another. The less unnecessary background noise we turn on, the more we can hear one another. The less "stuff" we have to care for, the more we can utilize our time and energy caring for one another. The more nurtured we feel by the environment of our home, the more inner resources we will have to nurture others. When we care for our dwelling place as the sacred space it is, we hallow out a place in which our ears can be more attuned to the language of the Spirit. Our eyes are more able to see the presence of all that is holy around us. When our home is built with care and affection, the angels cannot stay away — for food is to us, as love is to the angels.

Simple Rituals and Blessings to Create a Sanctuary of Family Life

Walking Gently

The way we enter our homes says a great deal about what we create within them. Some friends of mine revived the old Japanese custom of removing their shoes before entering the door of their home. They ask all visitors who are comfortable with the idea to do so as well. As a guest in their home, I recognize that this intimate space is quite sacred to my friends, and sense that our interactions there are positively affected by this simple gesture of humility. I have also found that a brief doorway blessing is another effective reminder to enter my home with care, so I wrote the following prayers:

Prayer Upon Entering

Spirit of Love, live in this dwelling,
Live in my listening, live in my telling,
Live in my seeing, with eyes of grace,
Spirit of Love, abide in this place.

House Blessing

God, may this house of wood and stone
be filled with love, become a home.

Soulful Symbols

Creating or choosing a symbol or work of art that reflects your family's faith and values is a fun way to acknowledge the deeper spiritual significance of your family relationships. Compose or choose a family song or poem, choose a family symbol which reflects particular qualities you wish to personify in your life together — perhaps a dove for peace or a sunflower for light and growth. You may also wish to work together to create an ongoing project, such as a family quilt made square-by-square or a family crest which depicts the beliefs and values your family holds dear. The possibilities are endless!

Naming Ourselves

When Andrew and I joined our paths in marriage, we decided to retain our birth names as one of our "middle" names and *choose* a family name to use as our last name. We searched through several name books, and finally decided to join two Hebrew names — meaning "heart of wisdom, compassion, and grace." Our family name is a daily reminder of some of the qualities we wish to personify in our relationships. Rather than making it a legal or public event, a family might choose a new name as a private symbol of identity. In many religious traditions, taking on a new name has great spiritual significance, and can be a powerful source of strength and inspiration.

Circle 'Round

Weekly or monthly family meetings can be an important way to create family unity, especially with older children who may feel a greater sense of "ownership" in family rules and goals if they have an opportunity to give their input. Perhaps the first part of your family gathering could be an enjoyable time for family members of all ages — to pray, sing, play games, work on a family project or express yourselves artistically. For the second part of the family meeting, younger children could be tucked in bed or asked to read quietly in their room while adults and older children (9 or 10, and older) converse about family issues that need tending. It's important to make it clear with children and teenagers that their ideas and opinions will be considered, and that the parents make final decisions on important issues. Family meetings are a good time to sing your family song, recall the meaning of your family name, display your family crest, or include other symbols that reflect your family faith, values, and visions.

Fond Farewell

When family members say farewell, whether for a special trip or in the morning before family members leave for work or school, sharing a parting blessing can be a source of inspiration and encouragement. I know one mom, who in her need to make the most of a busy schedule, says prayers with her children after everyone is seated in the car, ready to go off to school for the day. Before my children and their father venture off in the morning, we gather by the door for a verse or prayer. Our repertoire of blessings for "sending one another forth" includes the following Native American chants:

Go Gently

Go gently,
be pure,
be brave,
Be as humble as the earth,
and as radiant as the sun.

Longtime Sun

May the longtime sun shine upon you,
May all love surround you,
May the true light within you
guide your way home.

Welcome Home

The occasional times Andrew or I traveled out of town when our children were young, they greatly anticipated our return, and often went through elaborate preparations of card making and gift gathering to welcome us home. One summer, Andrew was away attending a teacher's conference for a week. As my daughters and I traveled to pick him up at the airport (cards and flowers in hand), Morgan, who was seven at the time, suggested that we create a "welcome home song" for the occasion. With her coaxing, the following song came forth. We practiced it in the airport parking ramp, and sang it to Andrew in the car before returning home. (Evidence that sacred moments can happen 'most anywhere.)

Sing through the repeated measures three or four times, beginning with a single voice, and adding voices with each repeat.

Personal Renewal: For Adults Only

Vision Meets Life

Write out your ideal visions of what you desire your home and family life to become over the next three years or so — but write it in the *present tense*, as if these visions are already being actualized! Perhaps you will want to consider your physical environment and financial situation, your relationship with each of your family members (including yourself), the atmosphere of your home, the ways your family celebrates the sacred and cultivates deeper spiritual connections, and the quality of relationships you create with friends, extended family, and the larger communities in your lives. Be as specific in describing your visions as possible.

Keep your written vision in a place you will see it, and remember to read it daily, weekly, or perhaps monthly (on the first day of the month, or the evening of the new or full moon). As you meditate on it, consider specific ways you can realize your vision. Also, consider making your vision part of your personal "new year" reflection each year — at the turn of the new year or as part of your birthday celebration. Read it, and consider tangible ways you have brought your vision "to life" during the year past. Modify it, if you need to, and consider ways you will actualize it in the year to come.

Our visions call for the use of our hands to work and our legs to walk about, lest our hearts and minds become heavy with the weight of our imaginings. Clarity is the unrippled pool upon which we may see our future. Yet, we may not stand there gazing too long, for we have a journey to make — a journey to that crossroads, where our present and our future meet.

2 ❧ A World of Dreams

The Sanctuary of Sleep

Oh, lightly, lightly tread!
A holy thing is sleep.

- Felicia Dorothea Hemans

Entering the Sanctuary of Sleep

By candlelight at bedtime one evening, I kneel beside the bed of my daughter, Morgan. Our bedtime ritual of prayer and song is silenced, as we are drawn into the magic of candlelight dancing across our faces, shining from our eyes. Suddenly, Morgan bursts into tears. When I ask why she is crying, she pours forth words of love for me, not unlike the way I did for her in the first few moments I held her after she was born. As we look into one another's faces, steeped in love, our relationship as mother and daughter is born anew. It feels as if we are meeting one another again for the first time, yet with a soulful familiarity that whispers of eternity.

I often pause to look into my children's faces, just before they slumber. In the dance of candlelight and shadow, I see beyond their tired smiles, their childish expressions. Just as I did on the day of each one's birth, holding their tiny body in my hands, I glimpse the largeness of their spirits, the greatness of the tasks they have come to the earth to fulfill. And I sense that when my children go to that holy, healing place called "sleep," where they journey with saints and angels, they will see their dreams in full view once again. No, not just their nightly tales of joy and woe, but the dreams that followed them here on the day of their birth, the dreams that follow them still, every day, as they wake once again upon the earth.

Wishing my children a good night's rest is a daily practice of letting go. Letting go the grasp I may sometimes, in my ignorance or fear, tighten 'round their unfolding souls. In these moments, I see myself more as their "foster mother" than the creative source from which they came. I am filled with the knowledge that these beings, these children so dear to my heart, are not my own to hold and keep. For each night they travel into the dreamy realm of sleep. There, they return to their true mother, who nurtures them as only the Divine Spirit can. She heals their wounds and anoints them for their earthly tasks in ways that my most loving gestures have only hinted at.

So I take care to "lightly, lightly tread," as I kiss my children in the candle-light. My heart expands with gratitude. God has entrusted me with so great a gift. I look into their glowing faces, and the silent prayer I breathe is this:

> A light divine shines from your eyes,
> O, may I never watch it die,
> Or serve to damp that heavenly shine,
> for you are God's more than you're mine.

Sleep well, children, remember well your dreams.

Ministering to Children in the Sanctuary of Sleep

I recall one winter night several years ago, when Andrew and I were both ill with a cold and flu. We could hardly drag ourselves around to care for *ourselves*, much less *our children*. We had recently moved to a new city, and had no close friends or family to call for reinforcements. Willa and Morgan were a great help, bringing us glasses of juice, fixing food, fetching a clean hanky when we needed it, playing quietly so we could rest.

The most nurturing of their get-well gestures came at bedtime. When we normally would have tucked them in bed and blessed them for the night, *they* became the "blessing givers." They tucked *us* in bed, stood in the center of the room with candles glowing, singing like angels. Few moments in my life as a parent have been so rich. It felt as if the hundreds of nighttime blessings they had received over the years were potently alive in the room. No doubt my daughters were priestesses. No doubt these blessings were breathing in them. No doubt the minutes we set aside each evening to sing and pray together had done more than settle them in for the night. They came boldly to meet the evening shadows. They came boldly to welcome sleep.

As Willa and Morgan sang to us, prayed with us on that winter evening, a myriad of memories visited me — my father, tucking me in at bedtime, reciting a silly poem that always made me giggle; my mother, singing me one last song before turning out the light. My parents knew these nightly comforts were significant, especially to a child who so resisted being alone in the dark.

As a young child, I sensed, though I had no words for it then, that each time I lay myself to rest, I must die a little death. Indeed, sleep has been called the "brother of death" — for we must, in a sense, "die" to this earthly plane, to enter again into the womb of sleep. This womb delivers us into the dream world of the spirit. For some children, the journey is familiar and welcome. For others, as for some adults, the journey is taken with resistance and hesitancy. Some children feel anxiety, confusion, even anger at a parent's coaxing, and their body's insistence, that they suffer this little, nightly death. Some children fight the need to leave their earthly home and family even for a moment.

As our children step into the gently rocking boat that carries them to the land of dreams, may we remind them that they are safe to cross that heavenly sea. May we let them know just as surely as we stand at the harbor to bless their departure, we will meet them again at that harbor to bless their return.

So let us see them off with prayers and songs that make them bold to meet their dreams. Let us give them reason to move toward the beauty of the evening with a welcoming heart. Then, when the morning sun opens up the sky, giving passage to their return, they will have eaten well in that land of deep slumber. For sleep, as much as any spiritual food, nourishes the souls of our children, strengthens their spirits for another day of living.

Seeking Wisdom in Sleep

Settling Into the Evening

As I have witnessed the significance of sleep to a child's soulful growth and well-being, my reverence for the evening hours of our family's life has also grown. No longer do I think of bedtime preparations as putting on pajamas, brushing teeth, or going "potty" one last time — although all of these can be an important part of a nightly bedtime routine. I have realized that the atmosphere of our evening has a great affect on the manner in which my children make the transition to their nightly rest.

If we think of the activities of our day as one long exhalation, and sleep as a deep in-breath, we can sense the importance of making the transition in a gentle way. We see the importance of slowing ourselves down in these evening hours, turning off the television and radio, creating space to simply *be* with one another in the coziness of our home. In this way, we can more easily assimilate all we have experienced in our day. Children have fewer filters than we adults do to protect themselves from the unending stimuli that comes at them throughout the day, and they greatly need this centering time before sleep.

During the school year, when bedtime is earlier, it can be helpful to make these evening hours from dinner on, your "home and family" time. Settling back into the family after a long day, can be just as important for children as having an opportunity to settle into bed. Of course, there will be occasions when family members will be "out and about" in the evening, and special events may inspire you to make an exception to your regular evening rhythm. Yet, if we strive to unclutter these hours, which prepare us for rest, we may with our children and the dear poet, William Wordsworth, claim "a beauteous evening, calm and free."

How Much is Enough?

Few topics arise as frequently in the parenting workshops I teach as the issue of young children "refusing" to go to bed at night. Frequently, the parents having the greatest problems with settling their children at night, are the ones who are shocked when they find out how early my children have gone to bed at various ages and stages. It seems many children who become overly *active* at bedtime are often children who are overly *tired*.

Finding the windows of opportunity to settle a child in bed easily may take a bit of intentional observation and planning. When my youngest daughter, Willa, started first grade (and let go her daily rest time), Andrew and I had to move her bedtime to 6:45! If we waited even 15 minutes to 7:00 (the school year bedtime we had planned for her), we found ourselves (all too often) having to deal with an overly active, whiny child. So, right around 6:45, the family gathered by Willa's bed for prayers, and by 7:00 she was tucked in snug for the night, lights out, her music box winding down its nightly song. Her third-grade sister, Morgan, who shared a bedroom with her then, went into our bedroom to read for 45 minutes. When Morgan climbed into her bed around 7:45, Willa was sound asleep.

Today, as many of us lead lives that are quite busy and active, it is essential for our children to get the rest they need. Sleep regenerates their life forces — physically, soulfully, and spiritually. It is a powerful balm in restoring health and wholeness in our lives. Dr. Richard Fried, an M.D. who spoke several years ago at the "Magical Years" parenting conference held at the Waldorf school in Ann Arbor, Michigan, gave the following guides in considering the sleep requirements of children: 8 months, 15 hours; 18 months, 14 hours; 4-6 years, 12 hours; 7 years, 11-12 hours; 10 years, 10 hours; 12-13 years, 9 hours; 14 and up, 8 hours.

Although these guides may seem extreme when we compare them to the sleep most children in our society are actually receiving, parents do well to consider their validity. I know many parents who have worked with these guidelines and (eventually) found that their children were healthier and happier when daily patterns were transformed to accommodate an afternoon nap or an earlier bedtime to promote a longer sleeping period.

To encourage more restful sleep, it is important to consider the environment of the child's sleeping area. Is it free of disturbing noises? Is it an uncluttered and nurturing environment? Is it warm enough in cool weather? It is especially important for children to be cozy and warm at night. In homes that are air conditioned, this can be as much of a problem in summer as in winter. Be sure your child wears warm enough pajamas. We keep our children's old cotton turtlenecks for them to wear with "long johns" when the weather is cool, (which it often is, here in Wisconsin). A warm sleeping bag can keep children from habitually kicking off covers. A hot water bottle can also be a warming bed companion on a cold winter night.

The healing balm of sufficient sleep is one of the most significant sanctuaries available to our children. Of course, we parents do well to follow the good doctor's guides to get plenty of sleep, too! In doing so, we wake more wise and rested, and ready for the new day.

Simple Rituals and Blessings to Create a Sanctuary of Sleep

Evensong

You may want to create a "family hour" just before your child's bedtime to enjoy an evening activity, such as singing, playing a board game, reading together, working on a craft project, talking about the events of your day. Last winter, after the dinner dishes were washed, our family often found ourselves cuddled in blankets in front of the fireplace, weaving a delightful, if somewhat sleepy, conversation. Children are often less needy at bedtime when they have shared some quality time with us during the evening.

Open Your Eyes

A simple way of acknowledging our affection for one another at bedtime is to gaze tenderly into each other's faces, and allow a feeling of acceptance and love to rise up through our eyes to bless our family members. When we nurture one another with "eyes of love," it has a profound affect on our relationships, for it reminds us of our deeper spiritual connections. When we pause in silence to see one another, we are reminded not to take one another's presence so very much for granted. Many a night at bedtime, our family members have gazed into one another's eyes, as we recite this verse I wrote for us:

> It is no little thing to look into your face,
> For there God's love is made real to me;
> It is no little thing for our eyes to embrace,
> For there we may glimpse eternity.

Touching Moments

Bedtime is a wonderful time to share the gifts of therapeutic massage with a child. A back rub, foot massage, even a face massage can help your child relax for sleep. My daughter, Willa, is quite slim and tends to get cold easily. So, one winter when she was going through a difficult time, I heated arnica oil and gave Willa a "tummy rub" after she crawled into bed each night. Another relaxing technique I sometimes use with my children, I learned from a friend who is a massage therapist. I have Willa or Morgan lie face down and I stand or kneel beside them. Placing my left palm on the left hip and my right palm on the right, I gently push their hips back and forth in a rhythmic motion. Have your partner or a friend try this technique on you, and you'll experience how deeply calming it can be. If you have never shared massage with your child, and want to brush up on some strokes, take a look at *The Modern Book of Massage* by Anne Kent Rush, listed in the "Healing" section of "Books and Resources," on page 146.

Nighttime Protectors

Consider the protective images that are reflected in your chosen spiritual path or faith tradition that may be a comfort for your child as they go to bed. Praying to God by whatever name, or a guardian angel, for protection and keeping, can help a child trust their spiritual connections. It is important, though, not to share images with your child that you do not believe in yourself. Children can sense our insincerity and unsureness, even when cloaked in the best of good intentions. (Of course, you may become more of a believer when your child describes to you a circle of angels dancing over her bed, as my daughter, Morgan, did for me when she was four.) The protective image you bring to your child can be something as simple as the protective wings of sleep, or the beams of a violet moon, as in the following song and poem I wrote to soothe my children at night. Consider also this simple traditional prayer:

"Angel of God, my guardian dear, to whom God's love commits me here,
Ever this night be at my side, to light, to guard, to rule and guide."

Sheltering Wings

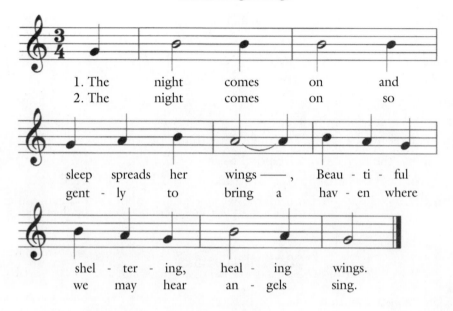

1. The night comes on and
2. The night comes on so

sleep spreads her wings ——, Beau - ti - ful
gent - ly to bring a hav - en where

shel - ter - ing, heal - ing wings.
we may hear an - gels sing.

This song was inspired by a poem written by Eliza Lee Follen:

> The night comes on,
> And sleep upon this little world of ours,
> Spreads out her sheltering, healing wings. . .

A Bedtime Blessing

O child, now lay your head to rest,
    another day is done,
A violet moon so peacefully
    becomes your nighttime sun,
And holds the place within you now
    that loves the light of day,
O child, now close your eyes, it's time
    star-babes come out to play.

Divine Conversation

It can be enlightening for a teenager to keep a journal each evening before sleep, in which to write their part of a conversation with a spiritual being — God (by whatever name), Christ, a guardian angel, a saint, or perhaps a loved one who has died — whatever spiritual being they sense most powerfully in their life. In the front of the journal can be written some open-ended phrases, such as: "A question I have. . .," "Something I am struggling with. . .," "A spiritual message or insight I received today. . .," and "Something for which I am grateful. . ." Each evening, the teenager can respond to one or all of these. Also, if they keep their journal by their bed, they can write about any dreams they recall when they wake in the morning — to consider what spiritual wisdom their dreams might hold.

Prayerful Pictures

The images children hold just before drifting off to sleep penetrate into them deeply over the course of the night. As part of your child's nightly bedtime ritual, select a prayer, verse, or song which reflects "pictures" of your child filled with wisdom, love, and a sense of serving others. These images can allow the child to feel a greater sense of purpose and love for the world as they wake in the morning to meet their work and play. One such prayer I wrote that has been meaningful for our family, is the following:

Bedtime Prayer

Blessed, Heavenly Sky that be,
Spirit of God who dwells in me,*
O, like the stars that shine this night,
So may I shine with wisdom's light,
So may I glow with love for all,
So may I help the great and small;
And now, as I lay down to rest,
May this good sleep be Spirit-blessed.

* For those on a Christian path, the first two lines may be changed to: "Blessed, Heavenly God that be, Spirit of Christ who dwells in me." In both versions, these first two lines speak of the experience of knowing the vastness of God's presence, at the same time one knows the intimate presence of God within.

Personal Renewal: For Adults Only

Sleeping Companions

As important as it is to consider what images children take to bed with them each night, it is important to consider the images that we, as parents, go to sleep with, as well. Do we find ourselves stewing over projects or situations "at the office"? Do we find ourselves flitting unconsciously through the dozens of household tasks that need doing before we can drop, exhausted, into bed? Do we find ourselves "vegging" with movies or TV shows which consistently reflect dishonest, careless, even violent relationships? Do we make a habit of watching the nightly news, which all too often reflects all that is wrong with the world?

To create a healthy sleep life, it is important to nourish ourselves with positive, healthy, spirit-filled views and images of the world in these evening hours. Whatever we choose to "take in" at this time of day will live with us deeply over the course of our sleep, and can affect our dream life and our ability (or inability) to commune with the Divine — a communion which is so accessible to us as we rest these weary bodies of ours.

Just before going to sleep is a good time to read through or meditate upon your personal visions of the realities you desire to create in your life. Reflect over the course of your day, and recognize in what specific ways your words, thoughts, and deeds were compatible (or inconsistent) with your visions. Also, if you are struggling in some way, or need enlightenment in some area of your life, this is a good time to pray for assistance. The mystery of sleep can be a powerful source of nourishment on our spiritual journeys — like drinking our fill from the communion cup that reminds us of our oneness with the Divine.

3 ∞ A Voice in the Wilderness

The Sanctuary of Nature

Each opening bud, and care-perfected seed,
Is a page, where we may read of God.

- Almira Lincoln Phelps

Entering the Sanctuary of Nature

There are nights I look at the moon and feel the Divine speak to me. There are days I hear God's voice in blades of grass or leaves on a tree. Not everyday. But then, I do not listen with my heart everyday, as I did more than three not-so-very-long decades ago, when the spirit of childhood hovered 'round me like an unending field of butterflies.

There is something in nature that calls us to be our most playful, noble, authentic selves. The natural world speaks to us in a language beyond words, a language that reveals to us the mysteries of life. Perhaps this is why children find nature so compelling. Perhaps this is why they can so easily transform a clump of scruffy shrubbery into a magical cave dwelling, lay quietly for moments on end to give honor to a ladybug crawling on their palm, squeal with delight at spying the first signs of lilies rising out of the ground in the spring.

My children have been some of the most inspired "naturalists" in my life, my greatest teachers in this ongoing discovery of the world. They remind me almost daily of the extraordinary joy one may find in a sunset melting across the sky, in the majesty found in a single flower.

When I was twelve, my family moved into an apartment building that stood across the street from a sunflower field. It was strangely out-of-place, for most of the land around us was filled with strip malls and office buildings. Yet, in the midst of all that workaday traffic, there stood, for a portion of the year, this shining sunflower field. I seldom saw anyone besides my sister and my friends in that place. I remember seeing adults there only once.

For me, as a child turning toward my youth, that field was a haven for contemplation and playful romping. It was an accessible patch of land where I could stand and look into the faces of those majestic, golden flowers, who seemed to be calling me to stand taller, be stronger. It was here in this sunflower field, the summer before eighth grade, that my friend, Maggie, and I made our friendship pact — that we would strive to make something of our lives, that somehow we would each try to make a difference in the world. And we promised one another that we would stand beside the other in our striving. No doubt we took our lessons from those glorious, golden friends, who stood so strong and tall in that very soil.

This is the way communing with nature affects me still. The only hitch is, I too often forget to make my daily journey to that sanctuary a priority. Fortunately, my children are here to show me the way. They do not seem to tire of coaxing me onto my belly from time to time, to crawl where the caterpillars have crawled.

And little by little, I am learning. I am feeling the voices of nature more often, calling me to give myself more playfully, nobly, authentically to this incredible, unfolding drama of existence. I am remembering to listen to the voice of God in sunflowers, ladybugs, blades of grass. I am discovering once again, that nature is bursting to share with us her wisdom. So, let us seek out forest wilderness and open field. Let us climb trees, roll in the grass, and look full into the face of every flower we meet. Let us take more time in our daily journey to set our hearts ablaze and infuse our minds with the glory of creation.

Ministering to Children in the Sanctuary of Nature

One July, a few years ago, when our family was visiting friends on a farm in Kentucky, we discovered a butterfly, who had just crawled from its cocoon, drying its wings in the slight summer breeze. After a few minutes, its shimmery blue wings quivered. Suddenly, it danced into the air, soared toward the treetops. Adults and children, alike, burst into applause. As we followed the butterfly with our eyes, our hearts soared skyward too. We thrilled in being witnesses to that very first flight.

Giving honor to such moments creates in us a more intimate bond with nature, allows us to see the earth and her inhabitants as kindred. When a child stretches his arms around a tree in the spring to quietly listen to the sap running through its veins, he cannot help but know the tree as the living, breathing being it is. When children tend to the birdfeeder all winter long, they cannot help but come to know the wild birds as their friends.

I recently heard a naturalist speak about the importance of encouraging children to deepen their relationship with nature. She said we are raising an entire generation of children who are quickly losing their connection with the glory of creation. There is a growing tendency for children to spend far more time in front of the television or computer than digging and planting in the earth, climbing trees, getting to know the native plants and wildflowers.

As parents and caregivers guiding this generation of children, let us seek out field and forest, where souls may be nourished with the earth's wild beauty. Let us explore lakes, rivers, state parks, farms near our homes. Let us plant more gardens, take more hikes, sit quietly on a hilltop to watch the sun make its dusky descent.

If you can't dig a garden, plant a flowerbox. If you can't find a forest nearby, climb a tree. If you have no nature preserve to explore, get to know the plants, trees, flowers, birds, insects right in your own yard, or along the street where you live, or in a neighborhood park.

Interestingly enough, my children have been the ones who have rekindled my wonder for nature, and now that my oldest daughter is journeying into the teen years, I am the one who often reminds her to open her eyes to the beauty of creation. As our children grow, and witness the adults in their lives communing with nature in ways they knew so well as young children, perhaps their childlike appreciation and wonder for nature's gifts need not fade with maturity. When they hear our awe-inspired exclamations for the beauty we find in the world around us, perhaps they will not hesitate to burst forth with joy for their own earthly discoveries.

Seeking Wisdom in Nature

Transformations

One rainy, cool summer evening, several years ago, I drove down our some-what busy street to run a quick errand. I was halted a half block away from our home. For there, in the middle of the road, was a jack rabbit who had obviously been hit by a motorist. One of its back legs was seriously injured, making it difficult for the rabbit to hop. Its eyes were wild with fright, its head and eye splotched with blood. I knew there was little hope of the poor creature surviving the blow. In the drizzle and stormy dark of the evening, I shooed the jack rabbit off the road, away from the traffic. Eventually my spouse, Andrew, brought the rabbit into our backyard, and gave it shelter where it could die in peace.

My daughters were ready for their nighttime story when this episode began to unfold, and though I hesitated at first to tell them about the jack rabbit, I knew that they intuited something significant was happening. Witnessing the rabbit's pain had affected me deeply, and I could see that Morgan and Willa sensed it. Worry was in their eyes.   So, very calmly and simply, I told them of the rabbit. Morgan's face immediately glazed over with unspoken questions: Would the rabbit live? Could we do something to *make* it survive?   Willa burst into tears, saying between sobs that she didn't want the "bunny" to die. I comforted them, and we prayed that the rabbit's pain would be relieved. Then we talked about how fortunate it was that I went out that evening, and that we were able to give the rabbit a place to die in peace. I told them that tomorrow we would plan a way to celebrate the rabbit's life and death.

As Andrew and I tucked our children in bed that night, I sensed that it was a privilege, in fact, for our family to share in this rabbit's death. It would be one of many opportunities to guide my children to embrace the gifts that death offers to all the world's creatures, including ourselves.

The next morning, we found the rabbit dead, lying under the shelter, just as Andrew had left it. Over the next few days, we planned our celebration, which included giving thanks for the rabbit's life, and returning the rabbit's body to the earth, where it could nourish the soil and plants. We sang songs in praise of creation. As my daughters placed stones and flowers on the rabbit's grave, there was joy in their faces, joy that would have been withheld from them if we had protected them from their grief.

Nature speaks to us of a partnership between life and death. Creation whispers to us that death is a sacred passageway. Wilting blossoms that fall before the fruit ripens. Compost that ages into rich, dark soil. Leaves that must fall in autumn, allowing the trees to gather their life forces to bring forth the new leaves of springtime. And yes, a "bunny," as Willa called it, whose broken, dead body is returned to the earth, where it may serve as food for the plants, that in turn, serve as food for the "bunnies." And thus, in the spirit of renewal and transformation, life cycles on. Life cycles on. . .

An Attitude of Gratitude

When we become more intimate with the natural world, as the Divine creation it is, we are inspired to show our appreciation and care for the earth, which provides such a bounty of goodness. From our example, children learn to express more openly their gratitude for the gifts we receive from the earth.

Consider nature's gifts that we experience in our own homes everyday — the meals we eat, the water we drink, the wood and stone used to build our houses and furniture. Consider clothing, bedsheets, blankets, and tablecloths made from cotton, rayon, linen, silk, and wool; reed baskets; wooden instruments; dishes made of clay and glass; pots and pans made of steel, iron, aluminum. Take a walk through your home with your children, and name the things you see that are made of natural materials we receive from the earth. Express your gratitude for these gifts. When your family sits to share a meal together, it can be a precious ritual to pause joyfully and give thanks with your children for the food provided. When you purchase or make a new item for your home, talk about the materials in the item which come from nature, and offer a prayer of thanks. Such reminders help us not to take these gifts for granted.

Children may also learn with us how to reciprocate for nature's gifts, by creating lifestyles that affect in positive ways the health and well-being of the earth and her creatures. Children will follow our lead in picking up litter, pre-cycling, recycling, and reusing materials and packaging, and avoiding the use of harsh chemicals and toxins in our homes and yards. A few simple words about not wanting "to dirty up the earth" will suffice when talking with very young ecologists. We need not burden them with the landfill problem, the ongoing pollution of our waters, or the poisoning of our soil.

During the first seven to nine years of life, it is especially important for children to build trust in the world as a good and beautiful place to be. By showing children harsh realities at a young age, we only serve to inspire a feeling of despair and fear in them. In the younger years, we can provide for them the "little picture" of how we may live from day to day in ways that make the world a cleaner, better place. The "bigger picture" can come as children mature, have greater resources to deal with these realities, and feel more able to affect a positive change in the larger communities of their lives. (Read more in-depth about this "age-appropriate" topic in Chapter 8, on "Serving Others.")

To discover ways you and your child can help to heal the earth, take a look at *Fifty Simple Things Kids Can Do to Save the Earth,* listed in the "Nature" section of "Books and Resources," on page 147. As you consider the effort it takes to make necessary changes in your lives, remember that you can make the changes one step at a time. See it as an evolving process of healing. Also, for inspiration, keep in mind the motto of one earth-friendly company, who quotes from the Great Law of the Iroquois Confederacy:

> "In our every deliberation, we must consider the impact
> of our decisions on the next seven generations."

Our children and our children's children deserve to know how to attend to the well-being of the planet upon which we walk each day. Through our example, may we teach them to walk with gentle steps that speak of healing.

Simple Rituals and Blessings to Create a Sanctuary of Nature

Naming the Days

A fun way to inspire family members to be more attentive to the daily events we observe in nature, is to keep a daily "nature calendar." You may wish to make your own, which displays monthly paintings or drawings made by family members. Each night before your child's bedtime, talk about observations or experiences you had with nature during the day. Decide together on a name for the day that reflects one of these events. Perhaps "The day of the first snow," "The day Willa met three fuzzy caterpillars," "The day we saw the sunset melt across the sky," "The day we went on a leaf hunt," "The day Jack Frost returned," "The day we buried the bunny," or "The day Morgan walked the swampy path." On the last day of the month, read through all the events one-by-one, and offer a prayer of thanks for all you have witnessed. At the end of the year, your calendar will make a wonderful addition to any "memory box."

Rainy Day Treasures

When Morgan was eighteen months old, Andrew and I took her on her first "rainwalk." It is an adventure for children to journey out into the wet to smell the earth in its freshness, and see how different the world looks in the shine and damp of gently falling rain. Creating intimacy with the earth means appreciating her in all of her moods, and finding joy in days that may, at first, appear to be less than ideal. Gather songs, verses, and prayers that celebrate rain. I wrote the following prayer and song for just such occasions:

In Praise of Rain

God of wet, damp, drizzly days,
We open mouths to sing your praise,
And drink, as do the fruit and grain,
of this, your gift, the precious rain.

Ripples of Rain

Rip - ples of rain, come dance with me, Come play, oh, sis - ter of the sea, Come wash me bro - ther of the dew, Rip - ples of rain, I will dance with you.

Walking in Nature's Shoes

To help your child develop more intimate bonds with the earth, practice becoming part of it together. Stand against the trunk of a tree or lay on a huge branch, and imagine how it would feel to *be* the tree. Lay on the ground and let your bodies melt into the earth, until you feel you are part of it. Sit on a huge rock by a lake, and become one with its strength, its stillness, its quiet. Joseph Cornell describes a wonderful game in his book, *Sharing Nature With Children,* in which participants lay on the forest floor, covered with leaves and pine needles. Camouflaged as part of the forest floor, children may experience animals and insects coming quite close. Seeing the world from nature's perspective can be enlightening and help us develop a more caring attitude for the earth.

Gift Exchange

Rather than assume with our children that nature is ours for the taking, it is a good idea to develop some sort of ritual of thanks when we pick up pine cones, cut flowers for a bouquet, or put a lovely shell in our pocket. There is a Native American tradition in which sweet sage or tobacco is offered to the earth when reaping her gifts. A special song or verse could be an offering of thanks. There are times, of course, when you are visiting state parks or nature preserves, when your child will need to abide by the "laws of the land," not to take anything dead or alive with them from that place. Here is a verse I wrote when my children were young, to remind them of such rules at a nature preserve we visited occasionally:

The Forest Wild

O, Journey with me child,
> into the forest wild,
Seeking earthly treasures
> we dare not steal away.

O, Journey with me child,
> into the forest wild,
And where we walk, dare not
> disturb the forest's wild way.

Inspired Tales

Reminisce over your childhood and youth, and consider moments that you communed intimately with nature. When my partner, Andrew, was 10 years old, his father took him and his siblings on a raft trip down the Colorado river. Andrew has told our children of his whitewater adventures, his daring climbs on the high rocks that border the river, sleeping on a slab of rock beneath the stars at the water's edge. The trip was one of the highlights of Andrew's childhood, and now he speaks of the Colorado river and their ultimate destination, the Grand Canyon, as he would talk of an old friend. Children thrive on hearing such stories again and again, because they live so deeply in us. Of course the stories you tell your children, of your intimate experiences with nature, need not be so dramatic. A simple story of spying a duck splashing in a puddle next to your house can also be captivating. When we relive moments of communion with nature through sharing our personal stories, our children not only gain a deeper appreciation for the beauty of nature, they also have the opportunity to get to know us, as the storyteller, more intimately.

Natural Adventures

As a teenager, it can be a powerful experience to participate in some sort of nature challenge. There is a Native American tradition called a "Vision Quest," that is a part of a youth's coming of age ceremony, in which the youth goes alone into the wilderness. On their quest, the youth receives a vision which they carry with them into adulthood. A teenager might participate in a "survival" camping trip with other youth (and well-trained adult guides), take a challenging rock climbing course, or go on a whitewater raft trip. As our oldest daughter is moving into her teen years, Andrew has found that participating with her in such adventures is a wonderful way to deepen the father-daughter bond.

Personal Renewal: For Adults Only

Walking the Wilderness Trail

As parents, busily meeting all the duties and responsibilities of family life, it is easy to forget to nurture our bonds with the earth, and thus, neglect one of our most accessible sources of personal renewal. Being in nature refreshes the body, renews the soul, airs out the mind. I know of one mother, at home with her children during weekdays, who hands over the responsibilities of parenting to her spouse when he returns home from work, while she takes a twenty minute walk. She says her brief daily ritual, being outdoors alone, without anyone asking anything of her, is a much cherished gift in the midst of a demanding day.

Make space in your week to commune alone with nature. Find walking trails near your home. If the forest, meadow, or park is not accessible, perhaps you can discover a nearby "street trail" in a quiet neighborhood where the trees are especially beautiful. You may also want to adopt a small piece of land close to home — a secluded patch in your own yard or at a nearby park. Visit the patch of land daily or weekly. Sit quietly and observe the plants, insects, and animals that make this patch of land their home. Observe the sky and the weather, the mood of the land on a particular day. You may want to write and draw in a journal as you commune with your special patch of land.

As we quiet ourselves to *be with* and observe nature, we create a space in our lives to observe more peacefully and objectively our inner being and relationships. When we open ourselves to all that nature has to teach us, we may receive a wealth of enlightenment and inspiration, for as Lydia Howard Sigourney claims: "Nature hath secret lore for those who lean upon her breast, with leisure in their soul."

4 ∞ Songs of Angels

The Sanctuary of Music

Everything that the sun shines on sings,
and sings of the Great Musician.

- John Harrington Edwards

Entering the Sanctuary of Music

Thanks to my mother, for whom singing was as necessary to daily life as eating and sleeping, I grew up with the gift of song weaving its golden thread through the days of my childhood. In those early years I learned not merely to sing, I learned to open the doors of my soul to music. I learned that music, as much as any experience I knew, could serve to thrill or heal me within, as if it were a visiting angel come to minister with joy or compassion.

I learned that when my mother sang to me, I could feel her love for me in every word. I learned that when I sang *with* her, that the golden thread of song wove a swift tapestry of affection between us. I sensed, as we lifted our voices together, that the Divine Spirit I call "God" sang with us, sang through us, was even, perhaps, the music itself.

Music continues to have such an affect on me. There are even times when I am singing that the physical world melts before my eyes, and I am surrounded once again by the misty substance of the spiritual. These mystical interludes are occasional and momentary, yet their impressions are lasting enough to show me that when we enter into the true musical experience, we are transformed by the mysteries of this Divine art, whether we are aware of it or not.

Music has the power to make us bold when we are fearful, joyful when we are in need of celebration. It has the power to comfort when we are in need of healing. Through the ages, we have called upon music to welcome babies into the world, to honor birthdays, to send forth the dying. With music, we lift our ritual into the realm of the sacred, for true music has the capacity to transport us, to allow us to commune intimately with the Divine in ourselves, in one another, in all of creation.

When I was in graduate school, a friend and I discovered a summer job in the underground subway of Chicago. Several days a week, we would hop on the elevated train in Evanston, where we lived, and ride along with a myriad of subway characters to eventually take our post at an underground subway stop as *street musicians*. It was that summer job that made it impossible for me to ever do work again for which I did not hold a deep passion.

As my friend strapped on her guitar, and we lifted our voices in sweet harmony, the herd of people before us, waiting for one more train on one more ordinary day, suddenly came alive. Lifeless eyes in hallow faces began to dance, to smile. There was an almost tangible bond that suddenly materialized between the bystanders, as folks seemed to become conscious that these were *real* people standing around them, not simply fixtures of their everyday lives.

Some folks threw off mundane expressions to join us in our song. Some folks tossed not only money into our open guitar case, but also flowers, handmade bracelets, notes that spoke of the ways our music had brought joy to their day. Once when a drunken man threatened us, a tiny man half his size stepped in to defend us, warding the giant off with his umbrella.

Most of the songs my friend and I sang were not what could be called overtly sacred, but it was obvious that many who heard our humble offerings of music, in the midst of that workaday existence, experienced the sacred qualities of music itself. True music touches some deep, vulnerable place inside us that reminds us, however subconsciously, that these human bodies of ours are formed with Divine hands. We sense that music is not something any of us "make," so much as it is something that streams to us, through us from beyond.

Rudolf Steiner, the founder of Waldorf education, once said that if more people would sing, there would be less crime in the world. Rage, hatred, deceit—such cannot live in the realm of true music. Music is the great healer, balancer, harmonizer. Indeed, if all the people of the earth set aside a few moments each day to lift our voices in song, we would find our homes and our world a more peaceful and loving place to be. If we were willing to bare our singing souls each day to our children, our partners, and our friends, we would discover that music is a profound inspiration for a healthy and joyful life together. So let us lift our voices upon that golden thread, that it may weave a tapestry of affection over all the earth.

Ministering to Children in the Sanctuary of Music

One of the most heartwarming moments I have experienced with my father, since I too became a parent, was the afternoon several years ago, when I walked into the room where he sat with my two daughters in his lap. He was reading them a story, and singing little, spontaneous songs to embellish the words that were written there. My heart melted at the sound of his singing, of his beautiful voice, so full of tenderness.

When I was a child, my father was far too shy of his voice to ever bare his singing soul to me or my siblings, except the *very* occasional times when he was coaxed by my mother, who was at the piano, to "ham it up" with a nostalgic rendition of "Danny Boy." Yet, here he was, his gift of song filling the room for his little granddaughters, and thus, for me. My eyes welled with tears as I looked into my daughters' expectant faces. They seemed to consider their grandfather's songs as natural a gift as his embraces.

I know a number of adults who have discovered their singing voices again after years of hiding them away — my partner, Andrew; my sister, Rebecca; a number of other parents, grandparents, and teachers. People who have been inspired by the knowledge that children learn from our example the freedom to sing openly and joyfully. Though the voices of these adventurous singers are a bit rusty with disuse, the music they offer is as beautiful to my ears as the songs of those often celebrated as gifted singers. For the *love* that has called them from their silence to experience true music once again can be heard in every tone. They are so willing to reveal that tender part of themselves that wishes to become one with pure song. This is what our children desire from us. Not perfectly polished canticles, but songs, simple songs, everyday songs that show them our love.

My children often ask, "Mom, sing the songs you sang when you were a child." And so we sing songs my mother sang to me when she was washing my hair or putting me to bed. We sing songs my childhood family bellowed as we traveled in the car together. We sing songs I learned from an old, energetic Sunday School teacher I had in kindergarten. Like my children, I am always delighted by these simple songs, songs that are like old friends bringing comfort and pleasure.

When I imagine my children full grown, and imagine the children in *their* lives asking them to sing the songs of their childhood, I consider it no less than a treasure that my children will have within them a mother lode of music to mine, placed there by the many musicians of their youth. Not all polished musicians, but musicians all the same. Grandparents, aunts, uncles, parents, friends, teachers who understand that we are all instruments upon which the musical tones of the universe beg to play.

Seeking Wisdom in Music

The Real Thing

I am saddened when I see a child waiting for their school bus in the morning, with a Walkman strapped to their head. Such children appear to have withdrawn to some inner space that makes it difficult for them to be aware of other people around them, the morning sky, the birds singing happily in the trees. It appears that such "music" is cutting the child off from the world, rather than serving as an inspiration for them to *commune* with the world, as *true* music does.

Our ability to reproduce music with electronic equipment has made available to us a wide variety of musical performance from around the world. Yet, it seems that our overuse of the Walkman, the boom box, the radio, the stereo is quickly dulling our ability to experience and create true music on a daily basis.

It is important to ask ourselves how we are assisting or inhibiting our children, and ourselves, in experiencing the healing, uplifting, enlivening impulses of music. Do our children experience daily the gift of song, lifted by live, human voices that may touch the soul in ways recorded music cannot? Do our children know the joy of playing a flute or harp, *creating their own music*, rather than passively listening to artificial, electronic sound?

One grandmother I know tells me that when her own children were teenagers, she and her spouse did not allow the children to play the radio, stereo, or television in their common family spaces. The television was way off in a corner on the lower level where it wouldn't interrupt the flow of family life. Family members were encouraged to play their own instruments freely in common family spaces, and were asked to play electronic music in the privacy of their own rooms at a volume that wouldn't disturb others.

We live in a noisy, sometimes chaotic world in which we often struggle to attune our ears to the beautiful. "Music" born out of noise and chaos, can only produce more noise and chaos. Perhaps the first step, then, in deepening the authentic musical experience in our children's lives is to cultivate silence. Whatever our children may be telling us with their mouths, I imagine our children's souls are crying out for us to TURN OFF all the background noise we create with our artificially produced sounds.

Perhaps we could commit ourselves (for a week or a month) *not* to turn on the radio, the stereo, the CD player. Perhaps in the silence that is suddenly revealed, we will pick up that unused guitar sitting in the corner, or that flute stored away on a closet shelf. Perhaps we will dedicate ourselves to singing with our children each day. And in the interludes between, we can learn to grow quite comfortable with the inner stillness and silence that too often prompts us to reach for the radio dial or CD player — the silence out of which true music may rise up on its majestic wings.

The Unfolding Journey

It has been said that music is the language of the cosmos. Young children, so recently come to us from the spiritual world, are naturally drawn to musical tones. If we wished to give a baby a peaceful transition at birth, in addition to dimming the lights or preparing a "Leboyer bath," we might also greet the child with a beautiful chorus of live human voices, singing their canticle of welcome, or playing a sweet lullaby for the child upon the magical strings of a harp.

As parents and caregivers, our musical guidance involves more than helping our children choose an appropriate instrument to play, as soon as they are able to hold a violin or sit at the piano. Music is an impulse that lives strongly in children. As their guides, we can help them express the music they hear from within, music their whole being longs to sing.

The voice is the first instrument a child learns to play. Young children need no formal instruction here, they need merely to have the opportunity to experience, and imitate, the natural, joyful singing of the adults around them. Formal singing instruction is appropriate as a child moves toward the upper elementary school years. Yet, ideally, this instruction for the older child will continue to foster the natural joy and ease with which young children so often meet their musical creations.

Even those who do not consider themselves "singers" may teach children a great deal by following some simple guidelines:

(1) *Sing gently,* so you can produce tones without straining your voice, and so you hear your child's singing at least as well as you hear your own. Singing together can produce a deeper sense of listening to another, especially when we sing with the purpose of lifting our voices as one.

(2) *Explore singing in your higher register,* even if you are more comfortable with the low tones of the alto or bass. For some of us, the quality of our voices when we sing the higher tones, may not sound as rich to our ears, but such

singing will allow young children to sing in the range most appropriate for them. In the upper elementary grades, children can begin to explore their lower "chest voices," hopefully without losing their flexibility for the higher range.

(3) *Breathe naturally as you sing*, and allow for adequate breath to sing each phrase of a song without straining to get to the end of it. Taking some deep breaths and relaxing your body (before you begin singing) can be a great help. When you breathe during a song, do not gasp for breath. Keep your body relaxed, and simply drop your jaw between phrases. The air will naturally flow in.

(4) When first singing with your child, *choose simple songs that you can feel confident about sharing*. Practice the songs by yourself and learn them "by heart," so that when you sing them with your child, there is no hesitancy or inhibition lingering.

(5) *Choose songs and instruments that are appropriate for your child's age and stage of development*. In the younger years, it can be healing for a child to have a gentle-sounding instrument, such as a harp or a Choroi flute, rather than the stronger sounds of the piano or violin, which may overwhelm the child's senses. See the "Instruments" section in "Books and Resources," on page 153.

(6) *Learn the basics of simple musical notation*, which are less of a puzzle than one might expect. Most likely, you can teach yourself with the help of a good book, but it might also be enjoyable to call upon a willing musical friend to assist you.

(7) *Above all, have fun!* Singing need not be a chore, but a joy for all. When we judge ourselves or others for our lack of musical ability or knowledge, we close ourselves off from musical possibilities that have a way of rising up among us when we stop trying so hard to "make it perfect," and simply enter into the gift of the song.

Simple Rituals and Blessings to Create a Sanctuary of Music

Singing Through the Day

Enlivening your child's day with music doesn't require a special occasion. Choose a morning song, mealtime round, or bedtime lullaby to celebrate ordinary daily moments. My previous book, *Seven Times the Sun: Guiding Your Child Through the Rhythms of the Day*, includes a number of such simple songs, that we have sung with our children through the years. When Willa and Morgan were very young, an acquaintance who made a visit to our house said that she was surprised and delighted by our tendency to "sing about EVERYTHING!" She was even more surprised by the way our singing got our children's attention. Spontaneous little songs are so much more enjoyable and nurturing for young children (and parents) than the "barking" noise that too often flies from our mouths when we are trying to get a child to listen. Singing can work magic for encouraging the cooperation of a child under seven. For example, one may take a young child's coat from the closet, and handing it to the child, sing:

Wil - la may put on her coat, her hat and mit - tens too.

The Inner Ear

In singing together, lifting our voices as one requires us to listen to one another with our "inner" ear. Singing allows us not only to listen to one another's voice, but to one another's presence, to one another's very soul. Singing can be a profound tool to cultivate communication at a deeper level. Learn to utilize the gift of song as preparation for any meaningful conversation: at mealtime, before praying together, or before a family meeting. You will discover that singing helps to hallow out a space for a soulful sort of communion.

Instruments of Peace

Playing musical instruments that produce gentle, peaceful tones can provide calming moments for children. Depending on your child's age and interest, a kinderharp, a classical guitar, a Choroi flute, tone bars, or a lyre can provide them with an instrument that inspires peaceful interludes. Some of these instruments, such as the kinderharp and the Choroi flute, are simple to play, even for adults who have not had any musical training. Teaching children a few simple songs or guiding them to improvise their own songs can be a source of delight. For sources to obtain these instruments, see the "Instruments" section in "Books & Resources," on page 153.

Songfest

Create musical gatherings weekly or for special occasions, in which your family members can enjoy the gifts of group singing and performing for one another. You may wish to collate your own family songbook for such occasions, that can be divided in sections for particular holidays, birthdays, and the seasons. Be sure to include fun songs and favorites for everyday occasions, as well. You may wish to invite extended family members and friends to join you for a songfest occasionally. Have everyone bring a potluck dish, and create a feast of food *and* song. Such a gathering takes little preparation, and can serve to deepen relationships and provide a meaningful sense of community.

Over All the Earth

It can be enlightening to journey into the woods with a child, or to sit quietly in the backyard or a nearby park, and still ourselves long enough to discover all the musical sounds that greet us there: birds singing, animals chirping, a woodpecker tapping, the treetops humming in the wind. Listen deeply to the less obvious songs of the natural world. Imagine what music might be heard from a rock, a cloud, a caterpillar. During such interludes we may discover that creation is alive with music, as the following songs celebrate:

The Sounds of Song

Per - haps the Spir - it who made — all things, is

One who whis - tles, One who sings, for the

sounds I hear 'most all day long, O - ver

all the earth are the sounds — of song.

In My Heart

In my heart I hear mu - sic, shin-ing mu - sic

all a - round me, In my heart I hear mu - sic

shin - ing mu - sic, pure— and free, Pure and free,

pure and free, shin - ing mu - sic, pure— and free,

Pure and free, pure and free, shin - ing mu - sic

pure — and free.

Personal Renewal: For Adults Only

Finding Your Voice

There is something about singing for one another that can make us feel exposed and vulnerable. Perhaps this is why it is easier for many of us to buy our children bedtime tapes or a Walkman than it is for us to sing with them. Unfortunately, in younger years, many adults were labeled as one of those poor children who "cannot carry a tune," and thus, continue to live with this frozen image of their "inability" to sing. Even those who felt confident about their singing as a child, may have grown doubtful of their abilities, after years lacking in musical expression. It is important to create for ourselves safe places to explore the sounds of our own singing voice.

There is an old African saying, "If you can talk, you can sing." For many of us, the key is giving ourselves permission to be a singer, allowing ourselves to play with tone, as a young child would, free from our adult rules and expectations of the outcome.

When I was in Detroit for a teacher's conference several years ago, I had the adventurous pleasure of taking a workshop with Dina Winter, the music teacher at the Detroit Waldorf School. Dina is an accomplished singer, who has a gift for accepting others' voices as they are, at the same time she reflects to the singers with whom she interacts, a vision of our higher singing selves. Perhaps this is how each of us might aspire to listen to ourselves and one another — to hear so clearly the potential for the free, clear tone that we actually assist one another in achieving it.

If you are not yet comfortable singing alone or with others, set aside a few minutes of private time each day to explore and play with the gifts of song. Sing in the shower, or as you go on your daily walk. Make an adventure of humming while you wait in the checkout line at the grocery store. Sing when you are stuck in traffic. Sing softly. Sing boldly. Sing with joy. Sing when you are in need of healing. Become familiar with the beauty of the voice that so poignantly expresses your individuality — for the beauty is there, singing, singing, singing to be heard.

5 ∞ Word Magic

The Sanctuary of Poetry

Hear the voice of the Bard!
Who Present, Past, and Future sees,
Whose ears have heard
The Holy Word
That walked among the ancient trees.

- William Blake

Entering the Sanctuary of Poetry

As a child, I was my sister's constant observer, she being over four years my senior. So I didn't believe, for one moment, in the quiet, easygoing, sometimes shy Rebecca that others seemed to know and accept. The poems she wrote gave her away. For in her poetry, I heard her crystal voice, singing clear — her brave, strong voice whose poetic "music" moved the mountains of my heart. Rebecca was the bard of my childhood. She was the one who welcomed me into the sanctuary of poetry. The one who showed me how words put together "just so" had the power to carry me to places within my heart and imagination that I never knew existed.

Poetry continues to be a cherished companion. At times, reading words written by great poets, alive or long dead, famous or unknown, I tremble with the sense of uncovering some long lost portion of a sacred text — a text that reveals clues to the mysteries of the universe. My interludes with great poetry have given me the experience of piecing together a "holy book," discovered one poetic remnant at a time.

Some say that ancient religious celebrations were born from the womb of poetry, that poetry itself is perhaps one of the purest forms of worship. Poetry is a profound tool for expressing great wonder and exultation, for uncovering beauty in the most unexpected places, for illuminating the many and varied faces of truth. It is a lens by which we may come to intuit and know the presence of the Divine Spirit, the most subtle movements of creation, and the intricacies of the human heart.

In a children's book, called *Emily*, written by Michael Bedard, a portion of the life of the poet, Emily Dickinson, is revealed through the eyes of a neighbor child. When the young narrator asks her father "What is poetry?", her father replies, "Listen to Mother play (the piano). She practices and practices a piece, and sometimes magic happens and it seems the music starts to breathe. It sends a shiver through you. You can't explain it, really; it's a mystery. Well, when words do that, we call it poetry."

When we listen to "the voice of the Bard," we give audience to the Divine. When we lift our language through the ring, the rhyme, the wisdom of poetry, we give voice to the playful Spirit of the universe. We find that place between music and speech, where the word dances to a tune so bare that we are compelled to listen deeply. When we begin to see the world through the eyes of a poet, life becomes a prayer that is offered with every breath. The pulse of the universe becomes tangible to our ears, and is felt within the beating of our own heart.

Ministering to Children
in the Sanctuary of Poetry

When I was a child, my mother shared with me a poem from a James Whitcomb Riley collection, called "Little Mahala Ashcraft." The opening (and closing) stanza of the poem comes back to me often:

> "Little Haly, little Haly," cheeps the robin in the tree,
> "Little Haly," sighs the clover, "Little Haly," moans the bee,
> "Little Haly, little Haly," calls the Kill-dee at twilight,
> And the katydids and crickets hollers "Haly" all the night.

This poem became one of the most cherished of my childhood. At first, it was not so much the message of the poem that I heard, but the music of it, the compelling rhythm and rhyme. With each reading, over months and years, I absorbed more fully the fact that "Little Haly" had died, and that it was her death that prompted all the earth and its creatures to call her name. As I grew older, and understood the feelings of the poem more deeply, each time I read it, I was filled with melancholy, torn heart strings. Yet, I returned to that poem again and again, asking for it to teach me of mortality, loss, grief, love:

> The medder 'pears to miss her, and the pathway through the grass,
> Whare the dewdrops ust to kiss her little bare feet as she passed,
> And the old pin in the gate-post seems to kindo'-sorto' doubt
> That Haly's little sunburnt hand'll ever pull it out.

Years later, when I was in high school, and my dear friend, Sheri, was killed in a car accident, these words ministered to me in a way little else could. For this poem, that I had carried with me through a good portion of my childhood, captured in its mournful stanzas the breadth of my grief. For months after Sheri died, everywhere I turned, I heard the whisperings of her name, saw her face. Even as everyone, including myself, seemed to go on with our everyday lives, I knew that the world would never look or sound quite the same again. It had been unalterably changed. And, at a time when most others found it uncomfortable and difficult to acknowledge my grief and offer comfort, I knew James Whitcomb Riley understood. Somehow, that made a difference.

Also, in those days following Sheri's death, my father wrote for me a poem. I was taken by complete surprise. I had no idea my father was capable of imbuing the written page with such beauty and feeling:

Oh what a lovely spring, sweet and fresh,
All dressed in beauty and glorious promises,
And time. . . and time. . .

Yet suddenly, without warning, winter has come,
And with it, unkept promises and shattered dreams.
The cold winds stab at the very depths of our hearts,
We shiver, as darkness and despair beckon us to defeat.

But wait my friend! Spring certainly wasn't for naught,
It was a wondrous victory. . .
Oh no, you have left us with the warmest of robes,
Memories, oh priceless, sweet memories.

You made yourself a part of us, and we will not let you go!
You will help light our way when it is dark,
You will bring us new strength when we are weary,
You will give us courage when we are afraid.
We will find joy from you when we are sad,
And we will have our quiet times together.

But even more, dear spring,
we will share the love and enthusiasm
your bright warm days gave so generously to us all.
Yes, my young friend, know as you now rest. . .
Spring lives eternal!
Until we meet again. . .*

* Written by Charles Bagbey, my dad, who now lives in Sun City, West, Arizona.

I realize now this poem allowed my father to say to me what he felt incapable of conveying to me verbally. I, also, could not find the words to let my father know what a balm this poem was to my soul, I only hope he knew then. I know he does now.

Goethe once wrote that we "ought every day to. . . read a good poem." I imagine he was pointing us toward the illuminating power one may find in all "good" poetry — for good and true poets have a way of giving us strength to meet our deepest fears, our hidden selves, to capture the beauty of simple, every-day observances, to feel and express our greatest moments of exultation. Good poets open the inlets of our hearts to healing.

So let us welcome poetry into our homes and families. Let us create with our children a "sacred book" that they may carry upon the pages of their hearts, and on the tips of their tongues. Let us fill this book with poems whose wisdom they may call upon whenever they need courage or comfort, whenever they wish to express some deep-seated joy. Oh, that each child might be blessed each day with the gift of good poetry, with the experience that words put together "just so" can carry us to holy places.

Seeking Wisdom in Poetry

Word Play

When I was in first grade, I was one of the slowest in my class to learn my ABC's. Oh, it wasn't that I didn't have an interest in language. No child's attention was more rapt when there was a poem being recited or a story being told. From my youngest years, I loved the way words play with one another. I often thank heavens my first grade teacher was not alarmed by my lack of "academic progress," and that my parents did not push me down literary roads I was not yet ready to travel.

What a shame that so many young children today are drilled on their ABC's, and handed ditto sheets to scribble upon daily, when they could be dancing to the poems of Langston Hughes, or reciting the little gems of Christina Rossetti, or hearing the delights of Robert Louis Stevenson. The natural way to learn language is to hear it, speak it, move with it. . . for language is most alive when it is *lifted from* the written page.

If we want children to develop a love of language, we'd do well to show them the way. As parents and caregivers, let us share with our children poems that speak to them (and to the child in us). Let us commit these poems to memory, so we may, when the occasion calls for it, spread them out like a veritable literary feast for all to enjoy. If we can help our children develop an inner delight and passion for language, there is little doubt that when the time is right, they will wish to unravel the mysteries of the written word. For all of time, it has been so.

Growing Poets

Poetry need not be overtly religious to speak to a child spiritually. It is often the poetry that tenderly guides us toward the Divine that can be most meaningful, and often has a more profound affect in revealing God's wisdom to us over time.

The first poems of childhood are the simple fingerplays and movement games of the baby and toddler. Which of us has not delighted with a youngster in the sheer joy of reciting Pat-a-Cake, Gaddyup Horsey, or This Little Piggy? The strong rhythms, physical movements, and repeated "surprise" of these poems of early childhood often bring squeals of delight from the babies and toddlers in our lives. In a culture sorely in need of more unrestrained laughter and spontaneous joy, who is to say such delightful play is not itself a kind of prayer? Jean Ingelow once wrote that "Joy is the grace we say to God."

As a child moves into the nursery and kindergarten years, the fingerplays and movement games become increasingly more complex. One example is "Flutterby," a fingerplay I included in my previous book, *Seven Times the Sun: Guiding Your Child Through the Rhythms of the Day*:

Words:	Movements:
	Start with hands crossed, palms facing you. Hook thumbs to create butterfly.
Don't flutter by butterfly,	Start butterfly in front of chest. Flap wings out and away to the right.
Come rest on my finger,	Make fist with left hand, extend pointer finger. Lay right palm on pointer. Flap right fingers up and down.
Come tickle my cheek,	Flap right fingers lightly against right cheek.
Come be my guest for the day or the week,	Left palm up in front of chest, start with right hand out and up to right. Flap right fingers and bring them slowly to hover over left palm.
But don't flutter. . .	Still flapping fingers, move right hand out and and up to right again.
Bye, butterfly.	Transform flapping fingers into a goodbye wave.

Young children will learn to recite poems simply by hearing them over and over again. Don't try to "teach" young children to memorize poetry. Simply share it with them consistently, and you may be surprised how quickly they begin to speak right along with you, reminding *you* when you have mistaken a single word!

When reciting longer poems with this age group, choose those with a story line, such as the old favorite, "Wynken, Blynken, and Nod," by Eugene Field, or A.A. Milne's poem, "Explained," in which a young girl is searching for someone who can tell her how God began. It is also nourishing for this age group to recite poems with a predictable refrain or phrasing pattern, such as "A Fairy Went A-Marketing," by Rose Fyleman, which is also a picture book.

In the first nine years of a child's life, use consistent, predictable rhythms in poetry. Throughout these early years, the rhythm and predictability that can be found in such poetry, deeply nourish a young child's strong need for rhythm and repetition in *all* of life.

Around 10 or 11, less rhythmic, free-verse poetry can be introduced, opening up a wide range of possibilities, including many poems from more contemporary bards. Yet, even at this age, it is important to remember that the strong rhythms of more predictable poetry can feed our universal need to experience the rhythmic pulse of life.

I smile when I drive up next to a car of teenagers at a stoplight, and am blasted with their body-penetrating rap "songs," pulsing from their car stereo. I am reminded that no matter our age, we all need rhythm and poetry in our lives, and will strive to get it any way we can. My prayer is that, as teenagers, my children will be equally as appreciative of Shakespeare, Hildegard of Bingen, May Sarton, and Robert Frost, as they are the pop poets of their day. And that the poets they have known through the years have helped them to find their own poetic voices. For, then they are at liberty to choose their own words and rhythms to express the stirrings of their bodies, souls, and spirits.

Simple Rituals and Blessings to Create a Sanctuary of Poetry

Familiar Refrain

Brief verses, spoken throughout the day, can turn potentially troublesome moments into playful interludes with a young child, and serve to delight and inspire children of all ages. A daily verse spoken together in the morning, at mealtime, or bedtime can create unity and peace in the family. This little trinket, from *The Book of a Thousand Poems*, might be used to guide a young child in putting on their shoes or boots:

> Pitty Patty Polt!
> Shoe the wild colt,
> Here a nail,
> There a nail,
> Pitty Patty Polt!

This mealtime verse that we frequently use is taken from a poem by William Butler Yeats, called "A Dialogue of Self and Soul":

> We must laugh and we must sing,
> We are blessed by everything,
> Everything we look upon is blessed.

To grace a family prayer time with older children (perhaps in the morning or evening), consider these words, written by Hildegard of Bingen:

> Good people,
> Most royal greening verdancy,
> Rooted in the Sun,
> You shine with radiant light.
> In this circle of earthly existence
> You shine so finely,
> It surpasses understanding.
> God hugs you.
> You are encircled in the arms
> of the mystery of God.

Poetry Partners

If your child shows an interest in composing verse, encourage them by purchasing a blank book or spiral notebook in which they may keep their finished poems. Of course, a younger child will need *you* to write them down. My daughter, Morgan, has had an affinity with poetry since she could speak. I learned that I had to keep pen and paper handy to catch the magic that often came spilling out of her mouth. With an older child or teenager, set aside time to write poetry together. Make a cup of herbal tea for each of you, choose a theme and a style (limerick, free verse, haiku, couplet), and give yourselves 30 minutes or so to write without interruption. Afterward, share your creations with one another. Depending on your passion for poetry, you could go on like this all afternoon!

Poets Are People Too

Choose a poet who appeals to children and adults alike, such as Langston Hughes, Robert Frost, or Emily Dickinson. Depending upon your child's age, select appropriate poems to recite together. Learn about the poet's life. If you are able, acquire a photograph or drawing of the poet. We discovered a wonderful children's picture book about Langston Hughes, called *Coming Home: From the Life of Langston Hughes*, by Floyd Cooper. Soon after, I ran across a whole collection of Langston's poetry compiled especially for children, called *Dreamkeepers*, and I was inspired to set to music excerpts from four of these poems for my nephew, Rion, for his 15th birthday. Since Rion lives hundreds of miles away, we recorded the song on a cassette tape and sent it to him. These excerpts are now engraved upon our memories, and Langston Hughes has become a household name. You might also consider creating a dramatic presentation with several poems from a particular poet for a special occasion. My children and I have staged such presentations as gifts for my spouse, Andrew, for Valentine's Day, Father's Day, and birthday celebrations. (Shel Silverstein's poems lend themselves quite well for such dramatic offerings, and are full of humor and wisdom.)

The Gifted Poet

As one who has often written poems for those dear to me, I am deeply touched when others make the effort to gift me with the magic of their verse. These days, it seems few of us take the time to express our feelings and thoughts to one another in poetic language. Just as we may uncover our singing voices, so may we uncover our abilities to play with words, to express the nuances of our hearts and minds through poetry. The more we do it, the more easily the words and rhymes will come. One simple poetic gift is to write a poem using the letters of a child's name as the first letter of each line, so that the left margin spells their name, in what is called an "acrostic." I wrote the following poem for my daughter, Willa, when she was seven:

> **W**ispy, and wild to gallop, to run,
>   to throw her head back, and bask in the sun,
> **I**nto the day she enters so bold,
>   licking her lips of its life-stirring gold.
> **L**ight fills her eyes, and gladness her soul,
>   for life is a feast that she yearns to eat whole,
> **L**onging to meet equal strength from without,
>   the pony butts heads and tosses about,
> **A**nd yet when she stands eye-to-eye with the same,
>   she knows she can harbor her fiery flame.

When my older daughter, Morgan (whose middle name is "DeShea"), began to blossom toward her youth, I gifted her with the following acrostic poem:

Moving from childhood into her youth,
Opening now the treasures of truth,
Rose-lipped lassie, so fair of face,
Gold is her heart, pouring with grace
And honor, as if a priestess of old,
Now to learn honor is not to be sold.

Doors are for opening, choose them or not,
Each one a lesson not soon forgot,
Spirit now beckons the wise little maid,
Her girlish alliances never to fade,
Entreating her now, as her youth starts to shine,
Always honor yourself, for your Self is divine.

The Family Collection

Plan an occasional "poetry night," when each family member can bring a poem to share. The poem could be an original, or a favorite from some other bard. These poems could be read, recited, performed as drama or reader's theater, danced, or brought to life through simple gestures to accompany the spoken word. Young children may need your assistance in selecting a poem to bring. If they already know a poem "by heart," and are comfortable with the idea, encourage them to recite it. Otherwise, young children can simply watch and absorb the offerings of others. Gather all your family favorites in a binder, and create your own family poetry collection.

Personal Renewal: For Adults Only

A Poet in Your Pocket

I am fortunate that my sister, Rebecca, continues to write her poetry. From time to time, she sends me a bundle of it. I sit and read, and am moved to laughter and tears. We all need poets in our lives. If they are not readily available, we would do well to seek them out.

One of my favorite poets is Walt Whitman, not only for the quality of his poetry, but for his free and adventurous spirit. I appreciate his deep compassion for other human beings, which did not prevent him from bluntly offering his thinking, feelings, and opinions, as witnessed so poignantly in one of his most famous poems, Song of Myself.* For my 34th birthday, my partner, Andrew, gave me a framed copy of a photograph of Walt, with his long, white beard, earthy fashion, kind eyes. Every time I look at the photograph, his whole character reminds me to live with passion and sensibility, to be brave enough to pioneer new territories within myself, and within the world.

True poets have a great deal to teach us. If your life is not blessed with the wisdom of at least a handful of good poets, perhaps it is time to find some. Go to the library or bookstore and skim through some anthologies. Find the poems which speak to you, and look up the collections of these poets. Don't overlook the contemporary, local poets of your area. Working as a poet can be a lonely and little appreciated task. If there is a poet in your area whose work speaks to you, go out of your way to show your support — send notes of encouragement and ask them to let you know when they will be reading locally, so you can attend. Grow familiar with what it means to see the world through the eyes of a poet, and sure enough, one day you will wake up to discover that you can see poetry in the world through new eyes of your own.

---

* Adults who are Walt Whitman fans will appreciate the movie, *Beautiful Dreamers*. The film conveys a portion of Walt's life, as seen through the eyes of the director of a "mental institution," who strikes up a friendship with the poet when they discover similar philosophies about caring for the "mentally ill."

6 ∞ Telling Tales

The Sanctuary of Stories

If one but tell a thing well,
it moves on with undying voice,
and over the fruitful earth
and across the sea goes the bright gleam
of noble deeds ever unquenchable.

- Pindar

Entering the Sanctuary of Stories

When I was a child, I saw spirits that others around me did not see, heard voices that others did not hear. I was told that my eyes and ears deceived me, that my mind was "playing tricks." Yet, even now, the memories of those spirit images, those divine voices, are clear and real to me.

As a child of three or four, I told my mother that when I grew up, I wanted to be "a woman who goes to church," as other children might wish to be a lawyer or a teacher. No wonder I had this childish aspiration, for it was in church I heard stories so familiar to my own experience: folks being visited by angels, the voice of God speaking through a burning bush, Jesus turning water into wine. . . earthly improbabilities made spiritually possible.

These sacred stories helped me assimilate the spiritual "magic" so familiar to my childhood. They assured me that my "spiritual seeing" was not something of which to be embarrassed or ashamed. They affirmed my sense that Divine spirits were alive all around me.

As a child, my abilities to see and hear into the spiritual world were not exceptional. Many children relate similar experiences, if given the opportunity. Indeed, my own children have related to me visions of angels and spirits, heard voices I did not comprehend. But, many children learn to suppress their spiritual perceptions, living as they do in a society in which the spiritual world is often feared, and not affirmed as an integral part of our contemporary, daily lives.

Fortunately, there is a language available to us, as parents and caregivers, that allows us to speak to a child's more dreamy, spiritually imbued world view, even if we have long become a stranger to it — a language which has been passed on to us from cultures of long ago, who were more open and attuned to spiritual realities than we generally are today. The language is that of folktale, myth, religious history recounted from a spiritual hilltop.

When we tell our children these ancient, sacred stories — whether from an accepted "holy book," or from the wealth of folktale, legend, and myth available to us, we are doing more than reflecting spiritual realities and moral truths in a language that children can readily digest. We are bathing our children with pictures that inspire them to develop imaginative powers — powers that may serve to transform the world with hope and compassion, as Margret Meyerkort claims in her article, "The Hidden Meaning in Fairy Tales," from the book *Lifeways: Working With Family Questions:*

> No *initiative* is possible without imagination, without seeing the potential for growth and development in a situation which others experience as static — and therefore hopeless. No *compassion* is possible without our imaginative realization of our friend's or neighbor's predicament. Nor can *love* flourish without it. . . To fall in love is easy. We are driven to it. To continue to love needs imagination.

So, let us guide our children toward spiritual wisdom through the ancient art of storytelling. And whatever other stories we tell our children, may they be many, let us remember that there is something mystical in the telling of a story that has been preserved over the course of centuries. A story whose truth, or humor, or insight runs so deeply to the core of our humanity that it has been remembered, spoken, lifted up literally millions of times over the course of human evolution. Let us continue to set our imaginations ablaze with the ancient fire of wisdom we find in the stories of old.

Ministering to Children in the Sanctuary of Stories

One of my grandfather's most cherished possessions was his big, old picture Bible. I remember sitting with him, in his rocking chair, on his front porch, that old Bible spread across our laps. The pictures were compelling, but not as compelling as my grandfather's passion when he told me those ancient stories — for they seemed to live in every fiber of his being.

My grandfather never spoke to me about his moral or religious beliefs, never explained the stories he told me, never pushed me to think about how these stories applied to my own life. He simply infused my imagination with word pictures that would go on living in me long after he died — pictures that held more eternal wisdom for me than his explanations would have.

"Pappaw," as I called him, had spent most of a lifetime considering how the truths of these stories applied to his own life, and I sense now that because he understood the meaning of these stories so well for himself, their deeper meaning lived vibrantly for me also. Not in an intellectual sort of way, but soulfully, spiritually, they became my inner guides. I know now, that Pappaw's stories would not have had such a great impact, if he was not the person I knew him to be.

For, there was another story Pappaw was telling me, whether he intended to or not. It was the story of his life as it unfolded from day to day. Just as we adults eagerly assess the actions and deeds of our growing children, so too do children eagerly assess the actions and deeds of the adults around them, if not with their heads, than certainly with their hearts.

My grandfather's life, even the subtlest nuances of it — the measured way his words were spoken when he was angry, the easy, joyful way he worked in his garden, the kindness that poured from his eyes when he looked into my face— each interlude with him wrote a chapter of the "memory book" I carry within me that contains not only the Bible stories my grandfather told me, but the "stories" I found in the way he lived his life.*

Of course, my grandfather was not a perfect man. He could be as mischievous and hard-to-live-with as any of us. But he was a man striving to live by his values and beliefs. He was a man who, for at least one little granddaughter, personified love, pure and simple. There is little in a child's unfolding life as powerful as the presence of an adult who, with the choices they make from day-to-day, in seemingly insignificant moments, creates a living picture of the wisdom reflected in their chosen faith. I know now that, as important as my grandfather's Bible stories were in my young life, it was more important that he understood them, believed in them, walked on the trail of their wisdom. Because, for me, the *real* story was my grandfather.

* Some of my fondest childhood memories of my grandfather are recounted in my children's picture book, *Grandpa's Garden*, published by Dawn Publications, Nevada City, California.

Seeking Wisdom in Stories

Which Tales to Tell?

When I was young, my father told me stories about when *he* "was a little girl." Listening to him talk of a time when he "was a young girl like me," tickled me with intrigue. It thrilled me with a mixture of silly absurdity and curiosity to hear what my father imagined for himself when he walked in *my* shoes.

Though a child's momentary pleasure of hearing a story may seem fleeting, the images of a tale are absorbed deeply and may serve as catalysts for a child's development — spiritually, intellectually, emotionally, socially. In selecting stories for children, we do well to consider a child's world view and stage of development.

Early childhood is a time children are learning to trust the world as a good and beautiful place to be — an especially important lesson, since the very young child experiences the whole world as an extension of themselves. With toddlers and preschoolers, this sense of the world can be nourished through simple, un-dramatic stories about nature — a squirrel gathering nuts in the fall to prepare for the cold winter, a flower growing from a little seed, an earthworm digging in the garden all winter to prepare the ground for planting in the spring. Such stories reflect to the child the goodness and wonder of creation, at a time the child generally feels "at one" with all the world. Brief nursery rhymes, story songs, simple, repetitive stories, and brief stories recounting our daily events are appropriate for sharing with 2- and 3-year-olds, as long as the stories reflect the ideally unencumbered, protected environment of this age group.

From the ages of four to nine, a child is deeply nourished by folktales that generally have some sort of obstacle or evil to overcome, and always end with a positive resolution. Such stories allow a child to inwardly experience the strength of our human capacities to overcome trials and tribulations, the forces of good working to banish evil, the positive transformations that may occur when we are diligent and courageous.

Folktales have the power to speak to our children in ways that our moral lectures or spiritual explanations never would, for the first sort of "thinking" that children cultivate is "picture-thinking," not the independent, analytical sort of thinking that we know so well as adults. Stories bring truths and lessons in images that the child can integrate and understand on a soulful level. The transformations that take place in pure folktales are a mirror of our inner development, since the characters in each story represent various aspects of our own souls.

Generally, the milder the problem and the subtler the evil in a folktale, the more appropriate it is for the younger child of four or five. The more complex the folktale, the greater the obstacles, and the more sinister the evil displayed, the more appropriate a story is for the child of eight or even nine, who is becoming more conscious of such forces in their everyday lives. In this gradual manner, a child is able to assimilate their dawning recognition of evil in a way that does not produce fear and impotence in them.

Through experiencing pure folktales, a child builds up a feeling of confidence and courage to meet obstacles and transform the destructive qualities they may discover in themselves or in the world around them, as they grow. At seven or eight, children also thrive on hearing the legendary stories of the saints who have served God, humanity, or creation in some sacrificial way, and whose lives reflect divine capacities.

Around the age of nine, when a child is gradually moving out of the childhood years and catching a glimpse of themselves as unique individuals walking into the years of their youth, in many ways, they are leaving the world of the folktale behind. Emotionally, children beyond this age have a greater capacity for integrating pain, sorrow, and suffering. Stories that children hear at this developmental stage, need not always end with the happy resolutions they heard in the tales of their younger years. Children around age nine are able to take in more complex tales of struggle in the human quest for freedom — themes of which the Torah and Old Testament are overflowing.

Consider such dramatic encounters as Abraham being instructed to spare his son, Isaac, on the mountain top, Jacob wrestling with the angel, Moses encountering the voice in the burning bush. Of course, many of the most poignant stories of the Old Testament center on the men; however, there is a wealth of dramatic stories about the females of the Old Testament, which come out of the tradition of the Jewish "midrash" — a story or folktale told as an interpretation of the original scripture. Around the same time, children are also deeply nourished by Native American legends which allow them to reconnect with the world of nature that they knew so intimately in their younger years.

From ages 10 to 12, when children are losing touch with the more spiritually imbued world of early childhood, they thrive on ancient mythology (such as Mayan, Greek, Norse, and Roman). Such myths depict humanity striving to remain connected with the many faces of the Divine, reflected in the Gods and Goddesses of various religious traditions, who often appear themselves in human form. This is a significant time to share with a child stories of the central figure of their own religious faith who serves as an extraordinary human vessel, through which others witness Divine powers and communication — Jesus and Siddhartha, to name two.

In a society in which genuine heroes (of either gender) are seldom evident, older children are also nourished by well-selected biographies which may serve as a child's heroic guides, and shed light on how an individual's choices can affect their particular human destiny.

The possibilities of stories to share with your child are endless. As you dig through collections, searching for appropriate stories to tell at bedtime, for a particular holiday, or to meet your child's present developmental needs, it's helpful to set aside stories for other occasions and needs as well. Begin a story file so it's easier to get your hands on certain tales when they're needed, or save stories for the future that are more appropriate for a year or two down the road. Also, collect stories with healing value — stories that may meet a child's needs at such times as the death of a loved one, the birth of a new sibling, or at some other challenging passage of life. For ideas, see the "Healing" section of "Books and Resources" on page 146.

Of course, all through a child's journey, they will thrive on stories we create for them out of our own imaginings — stories intended to speak to a unique child, at a unique place in their own unfolding biography. My father's "little girl" stories were his way of letting me know there had been other little girls who had gone before me, and met similar joys to relish and woes to overcome. One of the thrills of hearing such tales, of course, was imagining my father as one of them.

The Wonder of Age-Appropriate Stories

Some may wonder if following age-appropriate guides is really necessary, especially in the context of one's faith tradition, in which most parents and religious educators hope children will absorb the stories of their faith through all of their growing years, no matter what their age. It has been my desire, since my children were quite young, to discover ways for our own Christian faith to speak vibrantly to them at each stage of their Christian journey.

One decision Andrew and I made when our children were young, was *not* to share with them a detailed story of the cruxifiction until they were around nine. Instead, we shared symbolic stories of the Easter message, such as the caterpillar who spun a cocoon to become a beautiful butterfly. Although our children knew of Jesus' cruxifiction and resurrection, we did not share with them a detailed story of his violent death. Some of our more conservative Christian relatives found this odd, since to them the cruxifiction was the central message of Christianity.

We, however, emphasized Jesus' life and teachings with our children, until we felt they were old enough to take in the evil and violence which led to the death of this most precious spiritual guide in their lives. When our daughter, Morgan, faced the realities of Jesus' death, and wrote the following poem at age ten, I knew that our approach was well informed:

> Because of You
> "We weep, we weep," said the willows,
> "We weep, we weep," said the birds,
> "We weep, we weep, because of you,
>   O you, yes, you!"
>
> "We weep because you were hanged,
> and nailed, and bloodied,
> O bloodied, yes, bloodied.
> We died, yes, died, we died because of you.

"But then you rose, yes, rose,
You rose from the dead,
To our heart's joy!
Ah, life! O, life!
Now our hearts swell with life!
And we live, yes, live,
We live, because of you."

Few Easter poems have moved me as deeply with the joy of death transformed or the life-giving power of Christ's spiritual presence. Using well-selected stories that guide our children gently to discover such profound spiritual
truths for themselves as they mature, enables them to receive spiritual insight and
inspiration that our theological instruction might dampen. Such an experience
of spiritual enlightenment gently engraves upon a child's soul the knowledge that
we humans need no intermediary to receive spiritual messages from beyond.

Spinning Words into Gold

Less than a hundred years ago, storytelling was as common as television is today. With the growing focus on electronic media, storytelling has fallen disappointedly by the wayside. Television has become the "storyteller" of the masses. This two-dimensional screen, which is so proficient at disseminating information, and acts as our most common source of modern-day entertainment, also dulls a child's emotional, intellectual, and spiritual sensibilities.

To nurture children who are compassionate, clear thinkers and doers, and who are able to create intimate bonds with others, we do well to recognize how strongly we have, as a society, displaced human intimacy by an electronic screen. We do well to turn off "the tube" more frequently, and allow the spoken word to be liberated through live conversations and storytelling. Many parents, who have not been encouraged to cultivate the art of storytelling, feel at a loss to know how to begin spinning tales for their children. For those who need some direction, consider the following guides to get you started:

(1) *Begin by telling stories familiar to you* — stories of your own childhood, or stories about your child when they were younger. You could also make up a simple story about an adventure taken by the child's doll or stuffed animals. When you are ready to tell your child a less familiar story, begin with something brief, and take on longer tales as you become more comfortable with storytelling.

(2) *Choose a story appropriate for your child's age* (see pages 92-95). However, in the context of a family gathering, with children of various ages, choose a story that will be engaging for all, recognizing that some compromises will need to be made now and then. In selecting stories for our children, Andrew and I try to seek a balance of stories that contain strong male and female characters, especially those in which a child or youth is the main character. We also enjoy telling stories from a variety of cultures and traditions.

(3) *Memorize a story when you can, to allow the story to come to life from the written page.* Hearing a story without looking at illustrations frees a child's imagination. Occasionally when I don't have time to memorize a story I plan to tell to my children, I photocopy the story without illustrations, and then familiarize myself with the story enough that I am not glued to the page. Ever since my

children were quite young, I have also chosen age-appropriate chapter books to read to them. Of course, the stories Andrew and I have set to memory have been some of our children's favorites. With young children, these memorized stories can be told again and again, which makes the effort well worth it.

(4) *When memorizing a story, read the story several times*, so that you can memorize the sequence of events. Visualize the story as you read it. Contemplate the meaning of the tale on a soulful, spiritual level. It is especially helpful for memorization and understanding, to read a story just before drifting off to sleep. Don't worry about memorizing the words verbatim, but be sure to remember all the important elements and events of the story, and any recurring phrases or verses. With young children who thrive on repetition, strive to be consistent in the way you tell a story, since the child will hunger to hear a story just as it was "the time before."

(5) *As tempting as it can be, don't let your dramatic tendencies get in the way of a story*. If you know and understand a story, and visualize it in your mind's eye as you tell it, the proper nuance of tone and inflection, and the subtle changes of voice that naturally rise up as a particular character speaks, will allow the story to live more freely in a child's imagination. Overt dramatic gestures and extreme vocal variations as a story is told may actually hinder the inner "picturing" of your listeners, no matter what their ages. However, grade school children will thrive on a bit more "drama" as they mature.

(6) *Don't question a young child about a story they have heard, or force them to analyze it*. Allow a story to speak for itself. In this way, a child may inwardly absorb the deeper meaning of a story. With *older children*, well-chosen stories can lead to meaningful conversations that allow them, and us, to consider spiritual and moral truths more consciously. Don't spoil a good story by moralizing or lecturing to a child afterward. Allow the child to take the lead, and listen to their reflections thoughtfully.

(7) *Have fun, and be gentle on yourself as you explore your gifts as a storyteller.* The more you do it, the easier it gets!

Simple Rituals and Blessings to Create a Sanctuary of Stories

Getting Their Word's Worth

When a child is wounded emotionally, struggling in some way, or in need of guidance with their peers, a story can heal and direct a child in ways that our lectures and encouragements can't. When my daughter, Willa, was in kindergarten, she was one of the oldest children in a class of 3 1/2- to 6-year-olds. Many of the other children wished to play with her each day, but Willa often made room in her play for only one or two of the older children, causing the others to feel excluded. Instead of talking directly with her about it, I created the following story, which I told her at bedtime for three or four nights. The results, according to some of the other parents, were nigh miraculous:

Long, long ago, in a faraway land, there lived a royal princess. The princess had beautiful clothes to wear, and a beautiful castle to live in. She even had her very own pony, which she rode everyday, down to the meadow at the edge of the castle grounds. There she met many of the village children who also came there to play, for the meadow was one of the most beautiful in the land. Many of the children came each day just to get a glimpse of the princess, and to imagine what it must be like to be so beautiful and royal and have so many things. Some of the other children had only ragged clothes to wear, and no toys of their own.

Each day, when the princess came to the meadow, she would point to two of the bigger children, and say, "You! And you! You may play with me today, and if you wish, you may even take a little ride on my pony." And off she went with her chosen playmates, to gather flowers and romp about, while the other children looked on sadly, for they so longed for the princess to play with them. They so longed for a ride on the princess' little pony.

One day, the princess decided she would not go to the meadow, but would take a ride through the forest instead. As the pony was trotting along, it tripped, and the princess fell off the little pony, rolled down into a ditch, and suddenly found her foot lodged under the trunk of a tree that had fallen there. She whimpered and cried, but no one was near. What was worse, her pony ran off without her. The princess cried and cried for help. Finally, through the trees, she saw a boy and girl — two of the youngest children from the meadow whom she had never played with before. They were leading her pony, and when they found the princess, they said, "When we saw your little pony without you, we became frightened for you, and thought you might need our help."

The little boy and girl helped the princess free her foot from beneath the fallen tree. She was so grateful that she hugged each one, and set them upon her pony. Then she led them back to the meadow, where the other village children were playing. From that day on, whoever wished to have a ride on the princess' pony, was sure to get one, and the princess played with all the children and knew each one by name.

Youthful Expressions

With older children and teenagers, it can be fun to create a "family story circle," in which to share stories of your lives. Each gathering might have a different theme, such as: "A time when I felt especially close to God," "A nameless stranger, who taught me something important about life," "My most frightening memory," "My most embarrassing memory," "My greatest accomplishment," or "The greatest day in my life." This is a fun way to get to know one another more intimately. Such stories can bring interest to any family meeting, to balance more mundane business or difficulties you are trying to sort through. Be sure each storyteller has everyone else's focused attention. A "talking stick," from the Native American tradition, can be helpful here. The stick is passed around the circle, to remind everyone visually whose turn it is to speak. All others listen attentively. Of course, any object can take the place of a talking stick. Consider a heart-shaped stone, a cross, a small Buddha, a feather (which was a symbol for truth in ancient Egypt), or any object which holds spiritual meaning for your family.

Family Folklore

Though children of all ages will be enthused to hear stories of parents and grandparents in their younger years, it can be especially enlightening for older children and teenagers to piece together their family biography over generations past. Family stories can give a child a sense of the unique family stream of which they are a part, and help them recognize how past generations have affected the present, and in what ways their present generation is unique. Buy or make a scrapbook to preserve stories, pictures, mementos, and anecdotes you and your child collect about your family biography.

In the Moment

Several years ago, Andrew and I provided occasional childcare for a 3 1/2-year-old whom we were just beginning to know. His mother served as a tutor for a mentally challenged man who was learning to read, so she would drop her son off at our house for a few hours at a time. Her son had not been away from her much, and when she prepared to leave the first time, he began to scream, and cried that he didn't want her to go. She consoled him for awhile, but when she finally left, we were faced with a kicking, screaming child flailing around on our living room floor. On our piano, I spied our clay whistle, shaped as four people in a circle, talking with one another. Gently, I blew the whistle three times, which immediately got the little boy's attention. Then I began to tell the following story, as he lay quietly on the floor listening:

Once upon a time there was a village, and in this village all the mothers and fathers would go out into the fields to work each day. The grandparents and children would stay at home to keep the house and fix the dinner for the family to eat when the parents came home after their long days' work.

Each day, as the parents were walking off down the road toward the fields, the children would gather at the village well to fill their jars with water. While they were there, they would say to one another, "Oh, how sad my heart feels when mother and father go to work in the fields! Sometimes I feel that I could cry all day until they come home."

But one day, as they talked, a child spoke up, "I know!" she said, "Why don't we sing to our mothers and fathers, as they go off to work! Then all day in the fields, they will have our song to carry with them." And so the children sang. (I blew the whistle three times.) The parents turned when they heard the song, and waved at their children, saying, "All day we will carry your song in our hearts. Be well, children! We will be home soon."

By this time, my enthralled listener was standing by my side, so I handed him the whistle, and allowed him to blow it as well. After that, our story became the first thing we shared on each of his visits, and his favorite part, of course, was getting to blow the whistle. When you create a story "in the moment" like this, you may want to scribble it down afterward, so you can remember it more easily. The stories I created in this way when my children were young, were generally the ones they asked to hear again and again. Of course, an ongoing saga may take too much effort to write down, if each episode is to be told only once. One father I know, created a story for his sons about a family camping trip that continued with a new episode each night. Last time I heard, they were on the 121st day of the camping trip, and still going strong!

Sing-a-long

Creating a simple song to accompany a spoken story, can add beauty and interest, as well as serve to ease young listeners in and out of the imaginary world created in the telling. Here is a song I wrote to be sung at the beginning and end of the Grimms' tale, "The Star Talers:"

Silver and Gold

Sil - ver and gold, Sil - ver and gold,

Hear now the stor - y the stars — have told, of a

night that fell so dark— and cold, and a

girl who came forth brave — and bold,

Sil - ver and gold, Sil - ver and gold.

Personal Renewal: For Adults Only

The Child Within

Perhaps one of the most significant tools in our parenting is to remember what it was like to be a child and youth. Recalling memories of our childhood and teenage years allows us to heal old wounds, discover forgotten gifts, and gather childhood stories that we wish to pass on to our children. Significantly, remembering what it was like to be at the age and stage of a particular child in our life, allows us to develop empathy and insight for their joys and struggles, so that we might help to guide them with greater understanding.

You may wish to begin a journal to record for yourself some of your earliest memories and significant recollections of each year of your childhood and youth. Rather than proceeding chronologically, you could begin by recalling your life at the age of your child. Recall the home in which you lived, and write or draw a sketch of it in as much detail as you can. Sometimes, remembering your physical environment can jar some long-forgotten memories.

Consider the important people in your life at a certain age, the inner struggles you experienced, your spiritual insights and important encounters with the Divine, important events, the great joys and interests you held, what school you attended, what your teachers were like, what your significant faith community was like, or the obstacles you were striving to overcome. Create a "portrait" of yourself — through writing, painting, drawing, clay modeling, or whatever medium inspires you.

As you draw forth memories of your childhood and youth, or recognize an inability to do so, you may discover a need to seek counseling in resolving past issues and memories. Whether you choose to seek out a professional or lay counselor, or a clergy person, be sure the person you choose is knowledgeable and skillful in the art of counseling. Clergy have many areas of expertise which may or may not include helpful counseling skills. Be selective, but do not fail to get the help you need. And *do not make the mistake of using your child as a confessor or counselor.* Deal with the lessons of your biography *yourself,* before selecting age-appropriate stories to share with your child about troubling times in your life.

Unresolved issues from our childhood and youth have a way of living subconsciously in our relationships with our children and others, and can often become stumbling blocks to healthy development. When we are willing to take an honest look at our past and reap the gifts our biographies offer, we discover a multitude of lessons as human beings and as parents — lessons which may become powerful learning tools for our children as well.

Consider the stories from your childhood and youth that would delight, assist, or interest your child. As I have shared vignettes of my younger days with the children in my life, I have seen their eyes light up with a vision of me as "one of them." In the reflection of those visions, I have been reminded how alive and ready to bless that child is within me. Her wisdom calls out to me. Her life informs my own.

7 ∞ Sacred Conversations

The Sanctuary of Prayer

Why must people kneel to pray?
If I really wanted to pray I'll tell you what I'd do.
I'd go out into the great big field all alone
or into the deep, deep woods, and I'd look up into the sky —
up - up - up - into that lovely blue sky
that looks as if there was no end to its blueness.
And then I'd just *feel* a prayer.

- From *Anne of Green Gables*, by Lucy Maud Montgomery

Entering the Sanctuary of Prayer

Once I heard a minister tell a group of children, during a "children's sermon," that there are *two* ways to pray. I was all ears. I couldn't imagine what those two ways might be. The minister went on to say, and show, how we can pray reverently with our hands held together in front of us, *or* with our hands open and arms lifted skyward. An awkward look of questioning came across the faces of several children, especially my own daughters, who were in that attentive huddle, and were somewhat unfamiliar with the two prayerful gestures proposed to them.

In the unsure pause that followed, I wanted to jump from the pew where I was sitting, and dance the most jubilant prayer I could muster. I wanted to teach the children a prayerful song that they could carry with them. I wanted to tell them of prayers I have prayed while washing dishes, changing diapers, hugging someone dear to me.

I wanted to tell the children of prayers I have experienced while running races, writing words upon a page, digging in the dirt to plant seeds in a garden. I wanted to tell them of prayers expressed through great weeping, joyous laughter, hopeful, spirit-filled visions. I wanted to tell them that some of the most meaningful prayers I have known are the moments I simply quiet myself and listen for the voice of the Divine, who often speaks to me from within my own silence. I wanted these children not to be limited by the ailing imagination of this minister who offered them but two prayerful possibilities.

The minister finally asked the circle of children if they prayed at home in the ways he had described. His question rendered my own children speechless. I could understand that. Having remained in my pew, I silently giggled at the picture of this minister joining us in our home, with me leading my children in an energetic, prayerful dance through the living room. He may have been rendered speechless as well! For within our family, we have found that there are a multitude of ways to carry on conversations with the Divine. Sometimes we come to these conversations reverently, sometimes boldly, sometimes bowed in humility or grief, sometimes with spontaneous laughter spilling from our hearts.

Even so, I have found, in guiding my own children to experience meaning-ful prayer, that the use of particular prayer forms *can* serve well. A child kneeling beside their bed and holding their palms together in that well-known, traditional gesture, can help a child to feel the sacredness of such moments. Yet, it seems important to recognize that what we often call "prayer" is simply an acknowledg-ment of the sacred conversation that is going on in our souls *continually*. When we open ourselves to this sacred conversation in ordinary and extraordinary mo-ments, we recognize that prayer is not so much something we *do*, as it is a way of being, a way of listening, a way of seeing. This is our challenge then, as parents and caregivers, not to simply "teach our children to pray," but to guide them toward the wisdom that their *lives* may be a prayer, a living prayer.

Ministering to Children in the Sanctuary of Prayer

As a child of seven or eight, I remember one evening, settling into my chair at the dinner table, with my three siblings, mother, and father. My mother usually offered a spontaneous prayer for our dinner blessing, or bravely coaxed a prayer from one of my older brothers, who was occasionally willing. But tonight, before my mother could do such coaxing, and with a mixture of teasing and expectation in his voice, one of my brothers piped up, "Who's to say our prayer tonight?. . . Dad. . . Dad, why don't *you* do it?"

My older siblings were trying to hold back smiles and laughter. All I could feel was hope and anticipation. I had never heard my father pray before. I so longed to hear him "talk to God." What will he say, I wondered. What words will he use? I almost ached inside to hear my father speak to the world of the Spirit, to show me he believed in Divine things. My father hemmed and hawed, blushed a bit, and laughed some joking reply I have long forgotten. Disappointed, I realized that my father would step aside, let another offer our blessing. He didn't know *what* to say. Couldn't force himself to do it.

A decade passed before the longing I felt that evening, to witness my father in prayer, was finally satisfied. It was that poem (on page 77) that my father wrote for me after my friend, Sheri, died. Though many perceived my outer strength and acceptance of Sheri's death, I was stumbling in a void of loss and doubt. The significant adults in my life were stumbling as well, and could not find the words to ease my pain. But in the midst of that dark time, my father's poem confirmed for me that this man, my father, did indeed communicate with the world of the Spirit, did indeed believe in Divine things.

The poem my father wrote for me was not addressed to "God," yet it was as much a prayer as any I had ever experienced. My father had written for me an ode to life, to the eternal essence of my 16-year-old friend whom we could no longer see with our eyes, or embrace with our arms. In my father's words, he prayerfully spoke of the spiritual life by which Sheri's being had been transformed. He spoke of the spiritual union we could continue to experience with her. His faith, his acknowledgment of such spiritual possibilities encouraged me in my path toward healing, and gave me evidence that the most important man in my life had a living relationship with the Divine.

Children long to experience from us honest, heartfelt expressions of our faith in the more invisible world of the Spirit. So, we need not feel pressure to abide by forms and gestures of prayer that seem forced or superficial to us. We do well to find tangible, useful expressions of prayer, through which our children may witness our sincere belief. Praying for and with our children is not a matter of always finding the polished words, the perfect forms, displaying some sort of generic, unerring belief. Praying with our children means that what we *can* affirm about our spiritual connections, *we do*. That the words and gestures we *can* find to make tangible our communication with the Divine are offered freely and often. Who is to say that prayerful poems, moments of meditative silence, walks communing with nature are not experienced by our children as truer prayers than our more traditional forms? For it is not so much the *outer* form we choose that determines the potency of a prayer, but the *inner* gesture of our heart and soul.

Seeking Wisdom in Prayer

Embracing Our Spiritual Protectors

All my life, I have sensed a spirit-presence hovering around me, inspiring me with life visions, comforting me in my pain, protecting me in dangerous situations. Some people call this presence a "guardian angel." Some people say we each can have more than one. For those of us who believe in this sort of spiritual guardianship, it is natural for us to share such beliefs with our children. The picture of a "guardian angel" is easily understood and integrated even, or perhaps especially, by very young children. It is a natural gesture for young children to want to imagine and pray to their special, angelic protector.

Some parents tell me they cannot bring such a quaint picture to their child, since the idea of a "guardian angel" is highly questionable to them. They say that even *if* such spiritual guardians *do* exist, there is no guarantee their child's angel will protect him or her from the pain and suffering of life. They say to give their child this false sense of protection would be manipulative and dishonest. I understand their concern. The same could be true for any such "greater power" to whom we of the earth are inclined to pray. When we attempt to use Divine beings merely as bodyguards who shelter us from life's tribulations, we are sure to be disappointed.

Yet, children are deeply nourished by pictures of spiritual protectors who may "hold and keep" them through all their joys and struggles, their ordinary and extraordinary moments. They thrive on developing inner pictures of loving spiritual protectors who care for their well-being and development as they journey upon their life's path.

Encouraging our children to cultivate an intimate relationship with such a spiritual protector does *not* mean we do so in hopes that the spiritual protector will guard our children from the pains of life. Rather, it means we support our children to cultivate relationships of protection and security *on a spiritual level*, no matter what wounds they receive in body, heart, and mind. It means that spiritual healing is made more possible, no matter what injustices or traumas they endure, because our children have become familiar with realities that reach beyond our earthly existence. They have had the daily experience of strengthening and enriching their souls and spirits through prayerful communion with the Divine.

Some of us pray to God by a variety of names: Allah, Yahweh, Sophia – Mother of Wisdom, Father, Lord, Great Spirit, Mother, Creator of the Universe, Eternal Light, Spirit of Love. . . Some pray to angelic beings, saints, and holy incarnations: Michael, St. Brigid, Christ. . . Yet, for some of us, it is difficult to know to whom we are to pray. For some of us, our inner spiritual lives and the ways we define them are constantly evolving. Some of us imagine God as genderless, faceless, even formless Spirit. Overly defined images of the Divine may lack meaning. How may we describe in pictures and images what is indescribable?

Yet, our children think in pictures, and they can more fully and easily engage in conversation with Divine powers who are imaginatively alive for them. As parents and caregivers, we do well to find meaningful names and images for Divine presence in our lives, so we may share that presence with our children in more tangible ways. Children feel much more secure in meeting the changes and challenges of daily life, when they have cultivated faith in a "spiritual power" greater than themselves.

Of course, the names and images of the Divine we acknowledge in our families, as parents and caregivers, are those which will be most significant to our children — at least, for the first several years of their lives. A fact which causes some parents to share their pictures of "God" *less* openly, for fear of "indoctrinating" their child with their own beliefs.

Rest assured, there *will* come a time in your child's life, as they grow toward youth and adulthood, when they will question *everything* you have taught them. This is a normal part of healthy development. What is most important for a child before this time of questioning, is to experience adults in their personal life who have cultivated a deep faith in the spiritual world, and who are willing to share that faith in loving and appropriate ways. For, in basking in the spiritual devotion of their parents, grandparents, and other spiritual teachers, children gradually recognize in themselves a capacity for similar spiritual devotion.

So, if you don't believe in angels, strive to discover *someone* or *something* Divine in which you *can* believe. Believe in God, by whatever name, or believe in the eternal presence of the saints or in the transformative power of love. Believe in the creative forces of the universe. Believe in *something* spiritual that you can name, some "greater power" with whom you may lead your child to prayerfully commune. Believe. For the sake of your child's soul. Believe.

Feminine Faces of God

Before Morgan and Willa were born, Andrew and I considered together the names and images of God we could both relate to meaningfully, and desired to share with our, then future, children. One name we decided to use is "Divine Spirit," although we continue to use the more universally accepted name of "God" in our prayers and celebrations together. Yet, we were aware that the pictures of "God" in our culture, to which our children would be repeatedly exposed, are generally male-identified in the images of "Father" and "Lord." So we decided in order to complement such images, we would also include in our celebrations and prayers, images of "God" as "Mother."

Having two daughters, we are now especially aware of the importance for girls to see their femaleness reflected as a Divine quality, not as a physical form of which to be ashamed or afraid. If we choose to picture Divine presence in human forms, it seems imperative to the healthy development of our daughters and sons, in relating to both genders, that we picture Divine presence as a parent who may serve as "Father" *and* "Mother." We do well to embrace the Divine Spirit reflected in both our maleness *and* our femaleness, for our daughters and sons deserve to know that the light of the Divine may shine equally bright from within the goodness of their unique beings, be they female or male. Our culture's adherence to the image of God as "Father," does *indeed* require the curative female counterpart.

The Unfolding Journey of Prayer

From the time our children were toddlers, prayerful songs and verses at mealtimes and bedtime were our mainstay of "family prayer" — prayer in which *all* our family members could participate wholeheartedly. When our children were around the ages of five and three, Andrew and I also began whispering little, spontaneously spoken prayers at their bedtime, to which they listened attentively. These prayers were brief, only a few sentences, and they focused on pictures of our love surrounding friends and relatives, and thanks for specific blessings of our day. After some weeks, listening to Mom's and Dad's prayers, five-year-old Morgan began to utter prayers quite similar to those she had heard us speak, and a bit later, her younger sister, Willa, joined in.

As Morgan and Willa matured, each began to inspire our prayer times with utterings uniquely their own. Though we focused our prayers with them, in the early years, on comforting, loving images, which they could carry peacefully into sleep, Willa's prayers, around the age of six, began to consistently focus on a longing to feed the hungry, and shelter the homeless. Each night we continue to hear such prayers from Willa. It is a gratifying moment in prayer when a child is able to hear and articulate the stirrings of their own spirit. Witnessing such prayers, allows us, as parents and caregivers, to support children in bringing such prayerful visions to life within our family and our larger community. (A theme explored further in chapter 8 on "Serving Others.")

To assist our children in developing the capacity for articulating their own spontaneous, heartfelt prayers as they mature, we do well to first encourage them to participate in prayer *with* us, so that their initial experience of prayer is active and less self-conscious. Unison songs and verses are an especially effective mode of prayer for young children, as well as folks of all ages, because there is both a "speaking" and a "listening" that transpires, as we participate in song and poetry together.

In the younger years, parents and caregivers may utter spontaneous, spoken prayers *for* our children, before they are able to offer spontaneous prayers for themselves. Such prayers are more meaningful for children when we use imaginative words and pictures. We can speak of God's love shining on us and others like the rays of the sun, or wrapping 'round us like a blanket on a cold winter night. We can give thanks for the rain that feeds our garden and fills the little pool by our house, where the robins take their baths. We can speak of our child's angel, who hovers around their bed to watch over them as they sleep.

When a child is ready to speak prayers for themselves, it will most likely be as natural to them as breathing, for they will have our own prayers to build upon. As we pray for and with our children, it is important that we model prayers that do not include petty requests or that "tell God" what must be done about a particular situation. Children will greatly benefit from prayers which recognize Divine presence within each of us, and in all of creation — in the animals, the trees, the grass, the sun, the stars. This will help a child perceive Divine presence within and around them, as they go about their daily lives. Children also benefit from prayers which focus on the transformative power of love that lives within each of us, and prayers which affirm the capacity of spiritual beings to watch over, guide, and inspire us each day and night.

As children turn toward their youth, they may wish to utter their most heartfelt prayers when they are alone. If it becomes difficult for an older child or teenager to speak prayers openly in the larger family circle, respect their needs. Silent moments together, in which each family member may inwardly express their own prayer and listen for the stirrings of the Divine from within their own silence, may be one way to engage in meaningful family prayer, without invading an older child's need to experience prayer in privacy. You might encourage a teenager to keep a prayer journal, which will be respected as "off-limits" material by other family members. You could also help them create a "prayer table" in their room, or give them a "prayer box," as described in the following section, "Simple Rituals and Blessings to Create a Sanctuary of Prayer."

Simple Rituals and Blessings
to Create a Sanctuary of Prayer

A Prayerful Place

It can be inspiring to create a prayer table or altar in a quiet space of your home, to invite family members to gather there, in silent moments of meditation and prayer. The table or altar can be low to the ground, so you may sit on a prayer cushion, or kneel at it. Perhaps family members will gather at your prayer table at a special time each day, or perhaps individual family members will seek out this prayerful place when they need a few moments of centering or prayertime alone. Decorate your prayer table with flowers, a blessing bowl in which fresh water is kept, inspiring pictures and quotes, gifts of nature (a shell, a fallen leaf, a rock, a pine cone), or whatever seems appropriate. It might be helpful to leave a book or two of spiritual meditations or stories nearby, or a copy of your family's "holy book."

Prayable Moments

Perhaps you've heard of the "teachable moment." Well, there is the "prayable moment" as well — when the circumstances of the day inspire an opening in which it is quite natural to acknowledge our communion with the Divine. When you are out in nature or on a walk, and witness some magnificent or preciously subtle movement of creation, you pause to breathe a prayer of gratitude. While digging in the garden, you and your child offer a simple blessing for the seeds you are about to plant. After someone calls to tell you of a relative's illness, you light a candle with your child, and together, you picture the person surrounded by the healing presence of Divine love and light. When an older child is troubled about a decision they need to make, you guide them to pray about their situation, to ask for spiritual guidance, and encourage them to be observant of their dreams or spiritual messages they may intuit, as they go about their day. Let us guide our children, more easily and often, to the daily joy and enlightenment we can find through opening ourselves in prayer.

A Prayer Box

Several years ago, my spouse, Andrew, and I made a "prayer box" for my mother. Andrew constructed a simple pine box, approximately 12" x 10" x 8". I decopaged the top of the box with a Native American picture of Joseph, Mary, and the baby Jesus. Inside the box, I placed such gifts as a special cloth, a communion cup, some candles and a candle holder, matches, a small wooden cross, and a "prayer stone" (simply a smooth stone that fits nicely in the palm of one's hand). I also included a prayer journal, which was a blank book, in which I wrote, on scattered pages, special prayers, inspired quotes, scripture, and ideas for using each of the prayer tools in the box. With the brief explanation of each "prayer tool," I wrote a Bible verse. For example with the explanation of the prayer stone, I included the verse which begins "God is my rock and my salvation," and with the candle, "God's word is a lamp unto my feet, and a light unto my path." Most of the pages in the journal were left empty, so more prayers and reflections could be added. A prayer box could be a meaningful gift for a teenager on their birthday, confirmation, bar mitzvah, bat mitzvah, or graduation.

Open Your Eyes

Though it may be more effective and comfortable to close one's eyes in moments of deep prayer or meditation, in our family, we have found that it builds up our intimacy and affection to look into one another's faces when we pray together. In such moments, we may experience joy, sadness, love, reverence, or questioning in one another's prayers that might have otherwise gone unnoticed, if our eyes were closed and heads bowed. Whether your family chooses to pray with eyes open or closed, praying together is a deeply intimate act. Find ways to pray together that build up safety and confidence among you.

Without A Word

There are prayer and meditation forms that do not center upon the spoken word. In a society so fixated upon verbal communication, it seems important to cultivate the wordless prayer form. An older child or teenager may benefit from your guidance in the art of quiet meditation and deep breathing, if your family's spiritual practice embraces this sort of prayer form. We live in such busy times, it is difficult for us to slow down long enough to hear the stirrings of Divine presence in our daily lives. It takes a good deal of intentionality to set aside a daily quiet time, in which we may prayerfully commune. Children of all ages and religious backgrounds can benefit from silent moments of spiritual centering. With very young children, these quiet prayer times may begin simply by taking time each day to silently rock in a rocking chair together, or lie on the ground and look up into the leaves of a towering tree or the blueness of the sky. Silent, prayerful moments could also be observed before an evening meal. In our noisy, busy culture, it is a curative tool for a child to learn to quiet themselves within. Silence is the foundation upon which we may strengthen our ability to attune our "inner ears and eyes" to the sacred conversation that transpires, as we empty ourselves into quiet moments of prayer.

Love Feast

Sharing dinnertime together has been one of our family's most cherished and consistent daily rituals since our children were toddlers. It is a time to relate to one another the events of our day, in an atmosphere of care and interest. A family dinner, or any mealtime, observed as a priority of the day, can be a precious time for prayer and conversation, and an affirmation that at least once a day we care enough to remember who we are to one another. The following song is one of our mealtime blessings that serves to remind us of the spiritual significance of these moments:

Angels Dine Here

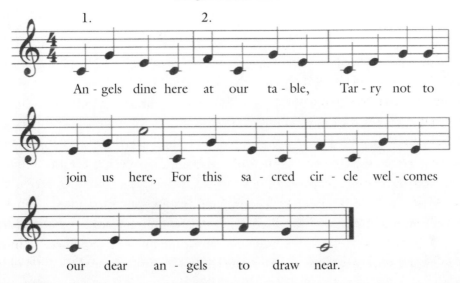

An - gels dine here at our ta - ble, Tar - ry not to join us here, For this sa - cred cir - cle wel - comes our dear an - gels to draw near.

'Round the Circle

With older children, "circle prayers," in which each family member is given an opportunity to offer brief, spontaneously spoken prayers, can be an encouraging way to include all family members as able and interested pray-ers. Young children, who are quite familiar with such circle prayers, may also be enthusiastic participants. However, it is important not to pressure a child to participate in such prayers. Simply, encourage all who *do* wish to participate. If you hold hands, those who wish to "pass," may simply squeeze the hand of the person next to them as you go around the circle. Such circle prayers may be concluded with a unison song or verse, such as this mealtime blessing:

> Mealtime Blessing
>
> Spirit, hear each word of thanks,
> each small request and great,
> And fill our hearts and souls with food
> not present on this plate.
> May the food of our affection,
> shared with these, so dear,
> Be worthy of the bounty
> we have spread before us here.

This blessing could also be spoken after a few moments of silent prayer.

Prayerful Gestures

As a liturgical dancer, bringing sacred dance to community worship, I am greatly aware of the healing and holiness one may encounter, when offering prayers through one's entire being — body and soul. Young children will be nourished by mirroring our own meaningful gestures which accompany a prayerful verse or song. The movements can be subtle and reverent, or full and energetic, depending upon the prayerful setting and intentions of the prayer. If your family members have never danced together before, play, sing, or speak a favorite song or poem, and encourage everyone to move to it simultaneously. Improvisation is a good warm-up for leading into choreographed gestures and movements. Improvisation is also a helpful tool for discovering meaningful movements and gestures for a particular song or prayer. Once your family members are comfortable moving together, you may want to co-create a choreographed dance. With older children and teenagers, it can be fun to divide a poem or prayer by giving each dancer a line or two to choreograph. Each dancer can speak the line to themselves and improvise until they find a movement that "feels right." After 5-10 minutes, everyone comes back together, and line by line, each choreographer teaches their movements to the others. Together the dancers decide how one section can move into the next. You might consider creating movements to the prayer by Hildegard of Bingen, on page 82, or the famous St. Francis prayer, included below:

> Make me an instrument of Thy peace,
> Where there is hatred, let me sow love;
> Where there is injury, pardon;
> Where there is doubt, faith;
> Where there is despair, hope;
> Where there is darkness, light;
> Where there is sadness, joy.
> O Divine (Spirit), grant that I may not
>   so much seek to be consoled, as to console;
> To be understood, as to understand;
> To be loved, as to love;
> For it is in giving that we receive;
> It is in pardoning that we are pardoned;
> And it is in dying that we are born to eternal life.

Personal Renewal: For Adults Only

Possibilities of Prayer

Prayer brings to the surface of our lives what our modern culture coaxes us daily to forget: that we are eternal. Prayer reminds us that our soul's journey does not end with death or begin with birth.

One would think we humans would be creating space in our lives to make prayer a priority, given the spiritual nourishment and assurance it provides. Yet, most of us find only a few brief moments a day, if that, to acknowledge our spiritual relationships in prayer. Sometimes I wonder if this is because we have made prayer such a serious business. We often come to prayer as some religious duty that is expected of us, and we fail to recognize prayer and meditation as the nourishing conversation it can be.

I wonder how differently many of us would come to the idea of setting aside a personal prayer time each day, if we began to picture it as an intimate daily rendezvous with a dear friend. I wonder what would happen if we considered all the possible ways we could build up our feelings of communion with that friend — through singing, dancing, chanting, sitting in silence, breathing, speaking earnestly what is on our hearts and in our souls, allowing ourselves to cry, even wail when our grief is intense, to laugh, even with abandon when our joy is great. I wonder what would happen if we brought to this time with our friend a bouquet of flowers, a poem, a story, a vision of the person we desire to become.

There are a myriad of prayerful possibilities, and the prayer forms one person enthusiastically embraces, another may find empty. We can each find the prayer forms that lead us to the prayerful path which is most inspiring for our unique spiritual journey. Let us remember that whether we are sitting, standing, kneeling, walking; whether we are singing, chanting, speaking aloud or silently within, reciting, writing, engaging in meditative exercises; whether we are working, playing, resting, embracing one another, visioning our future — we can experience transcendent moments that guide us toward the eternal within ourselves, the eternal beyond ourselves.

Which prayer forms have you utilized throughout your life — those you have been taught or have discovered on your own? Which prayer forms have most nourished you, and helped to build up your spiritual relationships? Which have not been helpful, or have even created barriers to spiritual deepening?

Take some quiet moments to consider what you feel to be the purpose of prayer. Who do you feel you are communing with in prayer? Can you "name" the spiritual beings with whom you communicate? What pictures have you embraced or created which help you to imagine these spiritual beings? How does prayer and meditation change you, and the way you respond to your life, your children, your spouse, your friends, your work outside the home?

If you have not yet cultivated meaningful prayer in your life, consider setting aside a few moments each day to experience prayer in a way you feel will be meaningful for you. And remember George Merideth's encouragement, that tells us: "Who rises from prayer a better (hu)man, (the) prayer is answered."

8 ∞ To Be of Use

The Sanctuary of Serving Others

Small service is true service while it lasts:
Of humblest friends, bright creature! scorn not one:
The daisy, by the shadow that it casts,
Protects the lingering dewdrop from the sun.

- William Wordsworth

Entering the Sanctuary of Serving Others

When I was in college, I had the opportunity to participate in the Appalachian Service Project, a ministry sponsored by the United Methodist Church, to help build and repair homes for low-income families who live in Appalachia. We had about 16 people from my hometown church on the trip, divided into three work crews.

My work crew consisted of two young adults and three high school students, and our job was to put up drywall in a cozy little home being built by a father and his eldest son. The house stood about 200 feet up the mountain from their main family house, and would become a home for the son, his wife, and their two children.

This family had three strapping older sons who were obviously capable of putting up the drywall. Mostly, they needed the supplies we brought with us each morning. But, as we worked side-by-side that week, we developed a rapport and affection for one another that went beyond our expectations. They wanted supplies, and they got them. They also received our labor, our interest, and our friendship.

We wanted to be of service that week, and we were. We were also the recipients of a multitude of gifts from this family of West Virginia. We ate lunch with them on their front porch each day, where we heard the father's delightful jokes and stories. We sang songs together — Appalachian songs unlike any we had ever heard before. They taught us how to shoot a rifle. We picked fresh vegetables from their garden. We played their version of mountain volleyball, and visited the coal mine where two of the older boys worked. For one week, we basked in the love of this family, whose respect and affection for one another was bold enough to receive strangers into their home.

At the end of the week, we were getting into our vehicle for the last time, saying good-bye, offering embraces all around, which took awhile, with their large family. It was time to go, and an awkward silence suddenly fell over the whole group. The father and I stood looking into one another's faces, our eyes misting over with tears, and then he said to us, "I only wish I was able to give to my children what your fathers have given to all of you."

The five of us immediately got lumps in our throats, thinking of the realities of our growing up years, in which our fathers spent most of their time working diligently to make what we considered "a decent living" for our families. I put my hand on this father's shoulder, and said, "Do *not* for one moment think that the material gifts we've received from our fathers are more valuable than the gifts you give to your children *everyday*." He pulled out a handkerchief to wipe his moist eyes, smiled, and nodded his understanding.

The five of us who drove away from that mountain home, on that summer afternoon, were not the same people we had been when we first came up that mountain a week earlier. We had experienced a transforming love with this West Virginia family — a love that transcends dialect, region, and social status. We went to "do good," to serve — and we found that we received in our service far more than we felt we had given. Indeed, with true service, it is commonly so.

Ministering to Children
in the Sanctuary of Serving Others

When I was a preschooler, we lived in a big, old house in Sterling, Illinois. The house sat on a two-acre lot that was bordered at the back by a railroad track. Trains often rushed by at the edge of that huge "backyard playground," and though I had heard stories of the so-called "hoboes" who rode on those trains from time to time, I had never seen one with my own eyes.

Then, one evening, I was helping to set the table for dinner. My dad was working late at the office, and my mother was caring for us four children. A knock came at the kitchen door, and when my mother opened it, there stood an old, skinny, sunburnt man, wearing tattered, dirty clothes. He asked my mother if he "might beg a plate of food." He looked as if he hadn't eaten for days. While he waited on the back porch, my mother loaded up a plate with a huge portion of our dinner — navy beans and cornbread. When he returned the plate, licked clean, my mother offered to give him work in exchange for food, if he found himself in need again.

That was the only time we ever saw the man. Yet, his face engraved itself on my memory. To my young eyes, his face was the face of hunger, tapping at our kitchen door — the same face who reminds me now that choosing to make healthy family life a priority does not keep us from serving the larger communities of our lives in ways both small and great.

When I was growing up, my mother didn't perform any great public acts of community service that I can remember. What I *do* remember is that during my preschool years, when the rest of my siblings were in grade school, mom cared for me with all the love and creativity a mother could muster. I also remember that when she knew of someone in need in our neighborhood, at church, and yes, at our kitchen door, she extended herself to help them time and again.

The memory of her feeding that old man a huge portion of our dinner when she had her own chorus of mouths to feed, made a far greater impression on my young heart than all the stories and admonitions my mother could have related to me about the importance of "feeding the hungry." I had an opportunity to witness her kindness and generosity in action.

As human creatures, we have been entrusted with life — to love, to heal, to serve the miracles of creation all around us. A difficult challenge in our contemporary culture, whose attitude is generally one of serving oneself, possessing things, using other beings for our own gain and pleasure. As spiritual sojourners, we are called to be vessels for the Spirit — human beings through whom Divine beings may work and play, and make their presence known in the world. This is, perhaps, the most important lesson to teach our children.

It is important to remember, as we identify needed changes on a global level, that the home is the place where attitudes are formed. Such issues as gender equity are nowhere more immediate than in the context of marriage and home life. Cultivating tolerance and understanding for people of other cultures, races, religions, economic classes is nowhere as transformative as in the intimacy of one's own home. In 1986, the United Methodist Bishops of the United States issued a pastoral letter, called *In Defense of Creation*, which says:

> The nurture of spirituality has its first and greatest opportunity in the intimate community of the family. Loving parents who share a visible reverence for God and creation, who cultivate shalom in all the relationships of the home and neighborhood, and whose work and witness in the world shine with moral integrity, are among the most powerful of all peacemakers. How a family demonstrates affection, shares power and responsibility, resolves conflicts, responds to hostility, copes with illness and injury, expresses grief, encourages achievement, conducts common meals, spends time and money, plans its vacation and travel, forms political opinions, confronts fears for the future, and worships or fails to worship God — these questions make the family the potential greenhouse of all peacemaking.

Though our work outside the home may receive less time and energy when our children are young, our commitment as parents to the intimate circle of family builds in us strength, wisdom, and compassion in ways no other training or experience can provide. Family life teaches us the true meaning of servanthood, and deepens the influence of our more public service a hundredfold. Those of us who make family life a priority, gradually find in the course of our everyday lives, that we have ample opportunity to serve others outside our immediate family circle, without neglecting those closest to us. The key, of course, while tending our hearth fires, is keeping our hearts and minds open to the tapping at the kitchen door.

Seeking Wisdom in Serving Others

It's a Small World

Most of us wouldn't consider attempting to teach a child to walk at six months or read at three years. We understand that in the course of a child's unfolding development, these skills will come. We know that early prompting from the adults in their lives can actually hinder a child from developing in these areas with ease and enthusiasm when the time is right. Yet, too often in recent years, we have taught our children of nuclear war before they have learned to resolve the "wars" that erupt with their own siblings or the neighbor child next door. We teach them of the landfill problem before they can say the word "pollution."

In a rapidly changing world, our own fears of the future often lead us to expose children to adult issues long before they have the ability to assimilate these issues in meaningful and helpful ways. When we thrust our adult world onto children, we create in them anxieties and pressures which make it difficult for them to develop as healthy human beings. We overwhelm them with their own sense of powerlessness to change all that has "gone wrong" with the world.

Consider the newly born, whose world is their mother's nipple and heartbeat, their daddy's voice, their sister's face, their brother's touch. The newly born — whose world is a dreamy swirl of color, shape, texture, sensation. Then the baby grows toward toddlerhood, becomes more physically active in discovering the world around them. No, not the world we adults know, but the world in which the child stands — the world which can be immediately touched, seen, heard, experienced, explored. As they grow, the child comes to know their unique circle of family life, the home in which they live, the yard or park in which they play.

Soon the child's world grows to include family friends, neighbors, extended family. Later, perhaps it's the church or synagogue community, the playgroup they attend with mom or dad, their preschool or kindergarten. Eventually, the child's world expands to the neighborhood, the grade school where the child is a student or the homeschooling community of which they are a part.

In the lower elementary years, the child gains a sense of the city, town, or county in which they live, and the state or province that is also included in their growing sense of "home." Most children gain a greater understanding of their home nation in upper elementary school as they learn geography. They begin to explore the relationships among nations and continents, and take in a greater understanding of this spherical mass we call "the Earth." In junior high and high school, the child's view of the world matures, for they are much more capable of thinking critically about issues that affect these larger communities of our lives.

When we consider the way in which the worldly consciousness of the child expands ever so gradually before them, we realize that teaching our children to serve those in the world around them, may be done most effectively when we consider what a child's world looks like at a particular age or stage in their development. By respecting a child's world view, we allow them, one step at a time, to grow confident in their abilities to be a contributing member of the "larger community," as they sense it. We allow them to grow familiar with the experience of making a difference in the world, by making a difference in *their* world.

<u>Serving As a Child's Guide</u>

Given a child's unfolding consciousness of the larger world, consider the following guides in nurturing a child's sense of service to others:

1) Encourage children to serve others within the circles of community already familiar to them.

For young children this begins in the home and family, with simple household tasks that grow increasingly more challenging, as the child develops new abilities for work. As a child's view expands to larger communities — the neighborhood, school, church or synagogue, consider ways you can encourage your child to serve in these community circles in ways appropriate for their stage of development. Working as a family or as a parent-child duo can be satisfying for those of all ages, especially a young child, who thrives on working side-by-side with an adult. Teenagers may find working with a peer group (at school, church, synagogue, or in your neighborhood) a great source of motivation. Working with other youth can be a catalyst for commitment.

2) Remember to guide children to serve communities other than the human kind.

The earth, plants, and animals are in need of our caring too. All of creation is sacred and worthy of our service. Again, begin close to home — caring for pets and houseplants, caring for your own yard or grandpa's garden, picking up trash at the neighborhood park or forest preserve you visit. By the time children graduate from high school, they will hopefully have a sense of how we human beings are stewards of *all* of creation, from our backyard to the expanses of our solar system.

3) Remember that television viewing and other media can expose children to adult issues they are not ready to assimilate.

Allowing children to *be* children, and protecting the innocence and wonder which are elements of healthy development in the first nine years of life, means shielding them from the barrage of adult information that comes pouring into our homes through written and electronic media. It is not necessary or healthy for a young child to be exposed to such adult concerns as a war being waged in another country, unless their lives are directly affected by it, such as when a family member is actually fighting in it. Hearing on the news of the murder of another child in your city promotes in a child fear and distrust about living in the world. No doubt, some children's lives are intimately touched by violence, war, and tragedy, shattering the innocence and wonder of early childhood. However, this reality is no reason to expose children unnecessarily to such events which do not directly affect their everyday lives. The more young children are exposed to such issues early on, the more overwhelmed and impotent they feel to face and transform such negative realities as they mature. Older children and teenagers are much more capable of processing the harsher realities of life that they will inevitably come to know, through their own experience or that of others. And they will, of course, need our support and understanding as they integrate such realities into their growing consciousness.

4) <u>Inform children about issues that require human service for which they have the power to change what needs changing.</u>

When a child first learns to read, we don't hand them a copy of *Treasure Island*. If we desire to teach a 6-year-old about caring for the environment, we pick up trash with them, teach them not to kill spiders or other insects, or use only a few squares of toilet paper at a time (instead of half the roll). A 10- or 11-year-old is much more able to "pitch in" their efforts with a school-wide or neighborhood recycling effort, and a 15- or 16-year-old to fully participate in a local youth group's efforts to change state laws that determine recycling, packaging, and waste disposal practices. It is also important to observe what issues a child or youth feels especially motivated to work on, and encourage them in that direction. A little bit of conviction can go a long way.

5) Balance serious intentions with humor and fun.

Community service need not be a drudgery, no matter how gloomy the picture. Consider how you can bring laughter and a sense of adventure to your work together. There is nothing that inspires a sense of community more graciously than sharing a good belly laugh. Also, balance your giving gestures with fun and nurturing for yourselves. Perhaps after rescuing native plants from a woods about to be bulldozed by so-called "developers," and transplanting them in your own yard, the whole family can go for a swim to relax and renew yourselves. Perhaps after a morning of visiting elderly folks who are bedridden, you can plan a yummy potluck lunch with your child's own spunky grandma and one of her friends. In so doing, we teach our children important lessons about self-care and renewal.

6) Strive to live in such a way that your lifestyle and daily choices serve the communities beyond your immediate family.

If we hope to teach our children to serve others in conscientious ways, it is important for us, as adults, to serve the world through the decisions we make and actions we take each day — where we choose to buy our food, what companies we finance through our purchases of goods and services, how we choose to invest our money, what detergents and cleaning products we use. Transforming our daily lives to reflect our deeper values of compassion and caring is a lifetime journey. We do well to take it a step at a time, recognizing that every change we make toward the good, is a step in the right direction. As our children mature into the teenage years, they yearn to discover adults in their lives who have the integrity to live boldly by their values and beliefs. Our example can be the inspiration they need to live with intention and integrity. (Of course, their way of doing so may be quite different from our own.) During the sometimes confusing and turbulent teenage years, helping a teenager discover the ways their gifts and interests may be used to serve others can give a teenager a profound sense of direction and purpose.

Welcoming Diversity into Our Lives

From the time our children are quite young, we can begin to foster a sense within them that they are global citizens, without pushing them to embrace a "worldly" consciousness they are not yet ready to assimilate. An important way for children to acquire tolerance and understanding for those of other races, religions, abilities, lifestyles, and economic classes, is to experience such people in the context of daily life.

Working to make our schools (both public and private) more integrated in the above areas can give children a wealth of experience with a variety of cultures, belief systems, and ways of being in the world. Seeking out opportunities to experience those who may worship, look, or live differently than we do, can be enriching for all involved.

When I was in high school, I was invited by the coach of a coed African-American track team to join them for their summer meets. A friend and I were the only Caucasian runners on the team, and two of the few Caucasian folks that ran in the track meets we attended. The friendships I developed with my teammates that summer were influential in breaking down some of my inner barriers about cultivating friendships with folks of other races and cultures.

Attending culturally-based performances, fests, and celebrations, seeking out multi-cultural faith communities, sharing a holiday or intimate celebration with a family who practices a different religion, cultivating a friendship with someone of a different race, or with someone who is unable to walk or who is blind — all of these gestures can shatter our stereotypes about those who are "different from us" in some way.

It can also be helpful to provide dolls for our children that reflect a variety of skin colors and cultures, and to include in our homes pictures of those from other races. Reading is another way to welcome a variety of folks into our homes, and may be a first step for children and parents whose immediate communities are lacking in diversity. As Lao-tzu taught so long ago — "The journey of a thousand miles must begin with a single step."

Simple Rituals and Blessings to Create a Sanctuary of Serving Others

Celebrating Service

It is important to acknowledge the ways we are served by our family members. We have created a Maundy Thursday ritual, as part of an attempt to create more meaningful Christian celebrations in our home, in which we wash one another's feet and name the ways we see each family member serving the others. The celebration is quite powerful and inspires tearful moments for all of us. Remembering to thank one another for daily acts of service we take for granted can encourage a greater sense of appreciation all 'round. Also, consider acknowledging your family's cooperative work before you begin it, or after some gesture of service is completed. You might stand in a circle holding hands and speak a verse together, such as this blessing from the work chapter of my book, *Seven Times the Sun:*

> There is a pause when work is done,
> A blessing for the task completed:
> I rejoice in the strength of my bones
> who welcomed labor as a guest.

Let's Party

A friend of mine has been the catalyst for an annual "block party" in her neighborhood, to foster a sense of community among her neighbors. She says it has really made a difference in folks relating to one another in positive and helpful ways when someone is in need. Find ways you and your child can get to know your neighbors better. If you are home with young children during the day, perhaps you can host a mid-morning brunch for the "at-home" parents and their children who live in your neighborhood. In our busy culture, it is easy for neighbors to feel extremely isolated from one another. Discover fun, creative ways to break down the invisible fences between folks in your neighborhood.

Caring to Share

There are a multitude of ways to extend the caring of home and family to friends, extended family members, and acquaintances. You may wish to set aside a few hours with your child each week or month to extend your care to those in need. Fixing a pot of soup for a sick neighbor, baking bread for grandma, doing childcare for a friend who has just gone through a divorce, doing laundry for someone who is going through chemotherapy. . . There are so many immediate opportunities for you and your child to work together to serve folks through the practical work of your hands. A few hours of assistance can go a long way in helping another person feel encouraged and supported. I will never forget the day our whole family was sick with colds and flu, and a friend of ours showed up on our doorstep with a big pot of chicken soup. (The love that went into her cooking was every bit as healing as the soup itself!) Also, consider cleaning up the trash in a neighborhood park on a weekly basis, visiting elderly "shut-ins" regularly (who are part of your church or synagogue community, or residents at a neighborhood senior citizen's home), planting a perennial garden at your child's school (with permission, of course), working together at a nearby soup kitchen, which provides meals for low-income folks, donating food or clothes to a nearby food pantry or clothes closet, or whatever opportunities arise. . .

Circle of Community

In our home, we have a "family wall," that is a collage of photographs of all the people we consider our "family community," some related by blood and some not. We consider ways we can deepen our relationships with these folks in more intentional ways — through visits, letter-writing, special celebrations and gatherings, etc. We also remember them in our evening prayers. Before her recent death, one of my adopted grandmothers kept snapshots and photographs of her "dear ones" on her refrigerator, so she would remember to pray for each of us everyday. What a source of inner strength this was, knowing that she was praying for us.

The Giving Gesture

In addition to giving of themselves, grade school children can be guided to serve by donating a portion of their allowance to an organization helping those in need. With a first or second grade child, you can suggest the organization to them. Consider Habitat for Humanity or an organization that works to feed the hungry. Housing and food are basic needs a young child can appreciate. Older children can make the choice themselves, but may need your help to consider the possibilities. You may also wish to create a bank for the whole family to save money for an organization your family wishes to support. Rather than dropping clothes donations at a donation center, my children and I recently took several boxes of clothes to a shelter, where we interacted with some of the folks who were staying there, and received a personal note of thanks. Such personal contact can make a deeper impression on children (and adults) about how our efforts of assistance affect others.

The Bigger Picture

With an older child or teenager, choose one area of your life, and for a whole year consider how your daily choices in that area affect others (locally and globally) — human beings, the natural environment, animals. Also consider how your choices affect your family's physical, soulful, and spiritual well-being. Perhaps you will want to look at your family's food choices, the use of electronic media, clothes purchases, lawn care, the work parents and teenagers are choosing to do outside the home, or your energy consumption. Consider changes that you desire to make as a family on a weekly, biweekly, or monthly basis, perhaps as part of a regular family meeting. Even by making one change a month for a year, your family can transform your lives in significant ways that enhance the quality of family life, while serving the larger world. For inspiration, following such conversations, you may wish to recite together these lines from William Wordsworth:

> "Enough, if something from our hands have power
> To live, to act, and serve the future hour."

Singing Servants

When I was a youngster in Sunday School, I learned songs about sharing Divine light and service with others. Those raised in the Christian church may remember these songs as well. . . "This Little Light of Mine," "Pass It On," and even (believe it or not) "Jesus Wants Me For a Sunbeam." Singing such songs can inspire children with vivid pictures of themselves as sharers of Divine light and love. Consider sharing with your child the following African-American spiritual:

Let Your Li'l Light Shine

Personal Renewal: For Adults Only

Opening to Community Life

To open ourselves to the larger communities of our lives consistently and lovingly, it is necessary to tend to that private, inner space within, which is so often neglected by those of us who parent. When I teach parenting workshops on establishing daily rhythms in the family, I find that the "rhythm" most consistently neglected by parents is that of our own personal renewal time each day.

I have noticed, over the past years, an increasing ability in the general population to create invisible walls between ourselves and others as we move about in public places — the grocery store, the post office, the gas station. Public interactions with "strangers" and "acquaintances" are too often lacking in warmth and interest. We so often fail even to look one another in the eyes. It appears that the busy, overstimulating lives we lead, make it almost necessary for us to create a shield around ourselves in order to keep any "extraneous" stimuli away. We have little room in our lives for others, because we have so little room for ourselves. We are, as a society, preoccupied with the superficial details of our lives.

Within our busy, oftentimes overstimulating days, we do well to find ways to empty ourselves inwardly, to gain clarity of heart and mind, to center ourselves within the stream of love that comes through us when we open ourselves to Divine inspiration. If more of us can find even a few minutes each day to remind ourselves of all that is truly significant in our lives — to remember that we are part of a magnificent universe, that we are not separate from others, but spiritually connected to every other being that exists, and that the strongest force for unifying all of creation is something as simple, yet transformative as love — I imagine those few moments each day will serve as a strong catalyst for helping to create a world in which peace is the norm rather than the exception.

Perhaps we are mistaken to think that it is our great and broad gestures of public service that have the greatest impact on our world. I cannot help but imagine that it is the small gestures: the way we live our lives each day, the quality of relationship we each have with our own self, the way we speak with our children, the subtle ways we encourage the cashier at the grocery store or the pizza delivery man. I cannot help but imagine the destiny of our planet hinges upon the way we choose to walk upon the earth, the way we speak to animals, touch trees, gaze upon flowers. I cannot help but think that the quality of all our simple, daily moments add up to far more than our greatest acts of philanthropy and our most publicly recognized gifts of service. If we are cultivating compassion and love in the smallest gestures of our lives, our greater gestures cannot help but be filled with the same.

And so we find, after all, that we are not so different from our children, that our soul's desire, every bit as much as theirs, is to discover the spiritual sanctuaries that help us find our "good and right relationship" with ourselves, our children, all of creation, beings seen and unseen. It appears that all things significant in life come full circle, as the seed to the harvest of seeds. Just as true service to the larger world, begins and ends in that still, small place within.

Books & Resources

Books To Nurture the Soul

In the book lists that follow, I have listed suggested age categories for those books which are more appropriate for older children, teenagers, and adults. This is due to the fact that many books set aside for younger readers have a wealth of wisdom for children, like me, who have grown old and tall. As a youth minister, I found that a well-selected children's picture book can serve well as a meditative tool for older youth, and as a mother, I have found that when I read with my children aloud, they are drawn into books that may seem too old or too young for them when reading on their own. When selecting books for your child, consider the guidelines for age-appropriate stories, found on pages 92-95. The books listed here which are intended for parents and caregivers to use as resource books are labeled "adult." This list is far from being complete. Use it as a springboard to search for books that will be meaningful to you and your family on your own spiritual journey.

Listed by subject (alphabetically)

Biographies

Anne Frank: The Diary of a Young Girl (10 & up)
> Anne Frank's life ended in a Nazi concentration camp in March of 1945, a few months shy of her sixteenth birthday. Two months later, Holland was liberated by the Allies. This diary, written during the two years before her arrest, when Anne's family was in hiding, has been called "one of the most moving personal documents to come out of World War II." (NY: Simon & Schuster, 1952)

Buddha by Demi
> The story of the young prince, Siddhartha, who leaves his palace to see human suffering for the first time. He leaves his family and wealth to go on a remarkable spiritual journey. (NY: Henry Holt, 1996)

Gandhi by Leonard Everett Fisher (8 & up)
> A concise biography of this great man's life, in a picture book format. (NY: Atheneum, 1995)

Happy Birthday, Martin Luther King by Jean Marzollo, Illustrated by J. Brian Pinkney
> A concise biography of the life of Martin Luther King, Jr., that relates the meaning of the day celebrated in his honor. (NY: Scholastic, 1993)

Minty: A Story of the Young Harriet Tubman by Alan Schroeder, Ill. by Brian Pinkney
> A glimpse into the childhood of this great woman. (NY: Dial Books, 1996)

Sadako and the Thousand Paper Cranes by Eleanor Coerr (9 & up)
> The story of a twelve-year-old girl who becomes ill with leukemia after being exposed to the radiation of the atom bomb at the age of two. A friend tells her the story of the crane: if a person folds 1000 cranes, the gods will make that person well again. Sadako folds six hundred and forty-four cranes before she dies. Sadako's spirit lives on, as her friends honor her life and death. . . (NY: Dell Publishing, 1977)

The Small Woman by Alan Burgess (12 & up)
> Gladys Aylward, as a young woman, travels alone from London into the heart of war-ravaged China with only a railway ticket, a few dollars, and a Bible. With humility and compassion, Gladys lives her Christian faith, a model which, to her astonishment, inspires even the Mandarin of her district to embrace Christianity. (Ann Arbor: Servant Books, 1985)

The Story of My Life by Helen Keller (12 & up)
> The extraordinary autobiography of Helen Keller, in which she shares the journey beyond her blindness and deafness, and discovers the living word. (NY: Scholastic, Inc., 1967)

See also: *Emily* and *Coming Home* (Poetry)*, and It's Our World Too!* (Serving Others)

Fairytales & Folktales

Best Loved Folktales of the World by Joanna Cole
(NY: Doubleday, 1982)

Heckedy Peg by Audrey Wood, Illustrated by Don Wood
A beautifully written and illustrated tale of good overcoming evil, as a mother rescues her children from the clutches of the evil Heckedy Peg. (San Diego: Harcourt, Brace, Jovanovich, 1987)

The Little Match Girl by Hans Christian Anderson, Illustrated by Rachel Isadora
An impoverished child wanders the streets selling matches on New Year's Eve. She is barefoot, hungry, and cold until she begins to light the matches and see glorious visions, that include her grandmother, who has died and who welcomes the child across the threshold of death. (NY: G.P. Putnam's Sons, 1987)

The People Could Fly: American Black Folktales by Virginia Hamilton (NY: Knopf, 1985)

The Rainbabies by Laura Krauss Melmed, Illustrated by Jim LaMarche
An exquisitely illustrated tale of a childless couple who discover a dozen tiny rainbabies after a spring rainfall. The couple overcome many obstacles to protect and care for the babies, and are finally blessed, by Mother Moonshower, with a child of their own to love. (New York: Lothrop, Lee & Sheperd, 1992)

Rapunzel by Barbara Rogasky, Illustrated by T. Schart Hyman (NY: Holiday House, 1982)

Saint George and the Dragon by Margaret Hodges, Illustrated by Trina Schart Hyman
(Boston: Little, Brown, and Company, 1984)

Snow White by Bernadette Watts (North-South Books, 1983)

Tatterhood and the Hobgoblins by Lauren Mills
Another beautifully illustrated tale in which good overcomes evil through the strength and courage of the ragged, wild princess, Tatterhood. (Boston: Little, Brown, and Co., 1993)

See also: *The Uses of Enchantment: The Meaning and Importance of Storytelling* (Storytelling)

Grandparent and Grandchild

Grandpa's Garden by Shea Darian, Illustrated by Karlyn Holman
The story of a grandfather and grandchild working side-by-side in Grandpa's garden. They learn firsthand of life, death, growth, and change. Includes simple gardening celebrations for breaking ground, harvesting, facing troubles and planting hopes. (Nevada City, CA: Dawn Publications, 1995)

How Far to Heaven by Chara M. Curtis, Illustrated by Alfred Currier
A grandmother and granddaughter slip out the back gate into the woods to discover how far away heaven is. (Bellevue, WA: Illumination Arts, 1993)

Through Grandpa's Eyes by Patricia MacLachlan, Illustrated by Deborah Kogan Ray
Grandpa's blindness is embraced as a gift, as grandpa teaches his grandson another way of seeing the world. (NY: Harper & Row, 1980)

The Whales' Song by Dyan Sheldon, Illustrated by Gary Blythe
Magical paintings reveal the story of Lilly's grandmother, who tells Lilly of the whales that sang to her when she was a child. Lilly believes her grandmother's story, despite the fact that Uncle Frederick dismisses the story as nonsense. Finally, Lilly discovers the whales' song for herself. (NY: Dial Books, 1990)

See also: *Annie and the Old One* (Healing), *Grandpa's Song* (Music), *Knots On a Counting Rope* (Storytelling), *By the Hanukkah Light* (Jewish), and *The Indian Way* (Native American)

Healing

Annie and the Old One by Miska Miles
The story of a Native American girl, whose grandmother relates that her own death will come when the blanket that the girl's mother is weaving on the loom is complete. The child tries to prevent her grandmother's death by unraveling the weaving, but her mother explains that many who are close to death have an intuition that tells them when it is their time to go, and eventually the child comes to peace with her grandmother's passing. (NY: Little, Brown, & Co., 1972)

The Bookfinder: A Guide to Children's Literature About the Needs and Problems of Youth 2-18 (Adult)
A helpful guide for adults to locate stories to help a child through a troubling time in their life. Topical index with full descriptions of each book. (Circle Pines, MN: American Guidance Service)

The Knee-Baby by Mary Jarrell
A gentle story of a child who gains a new sibling and thus becomes a "knee-baby" rather than a lap baby. Alan struggles to overcome his feelings of jealousy and isolation. (Take note that in the scene Alan almost begins to cry, that the line "These are bad signs," may be changed to "These are crying signs." (Toronto: Farrar Strauss & Giroux, 1973)

The Memory String by Eve Bunting
A child deals with her feelings of loss over her mother's death, as well as her feelings of jealousy about gaining a new stepmother. When the child breaks the "memory string" of buttons her mother had given to her, and loses one of the buttons, it becomes an opportunity for healing. (NY: Clarion Books, 2000)

The Modern Book of Massage by Anne Kent Rush (Adult)
This book has a section called "Vacations for Two," that contains simple massage techniques that only take a few minutes, and can be easily learned by children and adults alike. The other sections contain self-massage and relaxation exercises to renew yourself throughout the day. (NY: Dell Publishing, 1994)

The Tenth Good Thing About Barney by Judith Viorst
A child suffers the death of his cat, Barney, and finds healing through a funeral ritual created by his mom and dad. (NY: Macmillan, 1971)

Music

The First Song Ever Sung by Laura Krauss Melmed
In this gentle story, a little boy asks, "What was the first song ever sung?" Each answer he receives reflects the spirit of the speaker. (NY: Lothrop, Lee & Shepard, 1993)

Grandpa's Song by Brad Sneed
Grandpa is as big around as a kettle drum and has an enormous voice to match. His grandchildren are delighted by the way Grandpa finds every occasion to sing. Even though they sometimes have to plug their ears from the sheer volume of Grandpa's contributions, the play and humor Grandpa brings with his songs is irresistible. When Grandpa's memory begins to fail, the children bring healing through the very music Grandpa has shared with them. (NY: Dial Books for Young Readers, 1991)

Songs of the Earth: Music of the World by Anna Keloha (Adult)
A very welcoming collection of songs from many religious traditions, including African, Buddhist, Christian, Hindu, Sufi, Jewish, Native American, and Neoteric. (Berkley: Celestial Arts, 1989)

The Wonder of Lullabies and *Sing a Song of Seasons* by Mary Thienes-Schunemann
Former Waldorf music teacher, Mary Thienes, is creating a whole series of songbooks and CD's for adults to learn simple, beautiful songs to share with the children in their lives. This is a wonderful way for those who don't read music to learn songs quickly and easily. (Order from: Naturally You Can Sing, W2870 County Road ES, East Troy, WI, 53120, 262-642-5921)

Nature

Fifty Simple Things Kids Can Do to Save the Earth (8 & up)
Filled with experiments, facts, and activities. (Kansas City: Andrews & McMeel, 1990)

The Gardener by Sarah Stewart
Lydia Grace Finch brings a suitcase full of seeds, plenty of stationary, and a passion for gardening to the big gray city, where she must live with grumpy Uncle Jim for a time, while her mother and father find work. While she is there, she touches the lives of many with her hopeful attitude and her green thumb. (NY: Farrar, Straus, Giroux, 1997)

The Sense of Wonder by Rachel Carson (Adult)
Inspiration for adults to "help keep alive a child's inborn sense of wonder" for the natural world. (NY: Harper & Row, 1965)

Sharing Nature With Children by Joseph Cornell (Adult)
Nature awareness activities with an age-appropriate guide. (Nevada City: Dawn Publications, 1979)

Walk When the Moon is Full by F. Hamerstrom
Two farm children and their mother explore the beauty of nature on the night of each full moon. (Freedom, CA: Crossing Press, 1975)

Wild Country: Outdoor Poems for Young People
On this poetic journey to mountains, high country, forest, and sea, the grandeur of the earth and her creatures come alive! (Honesdale, PA: Wordsong, 1999)

See also: Grandparent and Grandchild (all), *The Tenth Good Thing about Barney* (Healing), *I Can Hear the Sun* (Serving Others), *Earth, Water, Fire, Air* (Multi-Faith), and Native American (all)

Poetry

The Book of a Thousand Poems: A Family Treasury
A seemingly endless collection to delight young children. (NY: Peter Bedrick Books, 1983)

Coming Home: From the Life of Langston Hughes by Floyd Cooper
A picture book that offers a glimpse into the childhood of Langston Hughes. (NY: Philomel, 1994)

The Dreamkeeper and Other Poems by Langston Hughes
A collection full of light and hope. (NY: Alfred A. Knopf, 1945)

Emily by Michael Bedard
A glimpse of Emily Dickinson, as seen through the eyes of a neighbor child. (NY: Doubleday, 1992)

Light-gathering Poems selected by Liz Rosenberg (9 & up)
Poems that inspire and bring forth light, with biographical notes on the poets. (NY: Henry Holt, 2000)

Prayers from the Ark and *The Creature's Choir* by Carmen Bernos De Gasztold
The profound simplicity of these poems, spoken through the voice of each animal, allows us to glimpse the character of each creature, and helps us to appreciate the unique being of each. (NY: Penguin, 1976)

See also: *Wild Country: Outdoor Poems for Young People* (Nature)

Prayer

Are You There God? It's Me, Margaret by Judy Blume (Ages 9-12)
A wonderful coming-of-age story for girls. In this realistic first-person narrative, Margaret struggles with feelings about menses, boys, friends, and faith. (Bradbury Press, 1970)

Earth Prayers from around the World edited by E. Roberts and E. Amidon (9 & up)
(San Francisco: HarperCollins, 1991)

Life Prayers from around the World edited by E. Roberts and E. Amidon (9 & up)
(San Francisco: HarperCollins, 1996)

The Always Prayer Shawl by Sheldon Oberman, Illustrations by Ted Lewin
A prayer shawl is handed down from grandfather to grandson in this story of Jewish tradition and the passing of generations. (Honesdale, PA: Caroline House, 1994)

See also: *Prayers from the Ark* (Poetry)

Serving Others

Frederick by Leo Lionni
A family of field mice gather food for the long winter, while Frederick gathers only sun rays, colors, and words! Despite their initial complaints about Frederick's obsession with the impractical, the mice find that Frederick's winter offerings are food for the soul. (NY: Alfred A. Knopf, 1967)

I Can Hear the Sun by Patricia Polacco
An intriguing story of a park attendant who befriends the ducks and the homeless people who come to the park. Many lives are touched when a homeless boy appears, and the others find that he has a special relationship with nature. (NY: Philomel, 1996)

It's Our World Too! by Phillip Hoose (10 & up)
True stories of young people, present and past, who have acted with courage and conviction to make the world a better place. (Boston: Little, Brown & Co., 1993)

The Legend of Indian Paintbrush by Tomie dePaulo
A story that affirms the importance of the arts, and the contributions of the artist to community life, as a boy struggles with the fact that he will never be a warrior. (NY: G.P. Putnam's Sons, 1988)

Miss Rumphius by Barbara Cooney
A delightful story of a woman who travels the world, and then ultimately discovers that her contribution to "make the world a better place" is by sowing wildflowers. (NY: Puffin, 1985)

My Great Aunt Arizona by Gloria Houston, Illustrated by Susan Condie Lamb
A story of a woman who does not travel the world as she dreamed, yet this woman finds her bliss teaching children in the classroom. A tribute to teachers. (NY: HarperCollins, 1992)

Wilfrid Gordon McDonald Partridge by Mem Fox, Illustrated by Julie Vivas
A young boy named Wilfrid is determined to help his aging friend, Miss Nancy, to find her memory. (Brooklyn: Kane Miller Book Publishers, 1985)

See also: The Gardener (Nature)

Sleep

Darkness and the Butterfly by Ann Grif
> A child who is afraid of the dark gets lost in the woods at night, but a wise woman and a yellow butterfly help her to find her way home and to overcome her fears. (NY: Little, Brown, & Co., 1987)

The Way to Start a Day by Byrd Baylor
> Rituals and traditions from around the world that celebrate early morning moments. This could be an especially helpful book for those who resist getting out of bed in the morning. (NY: Aladdin, 1986)

Storytelling

Aunt Flossie's Hats by Elizabeth Fitsgerald Howard, Illustrated by James Ransome
> Two girls visit their great-great Aunt Flossie, who has a colorful collection of hats, and a story to go with each. (NY: Scholastic, 1991)

Coyote and the Magic Words by Phyllis Root, Illustrated by Sandra Speidel
> A wonderful creation story, depicting a feminine image of the Maker-of-All-Things. This story highlights the special magic found in storytelling. (NY: Lothrop, Lee, & Shepard, 1993)

"The Hidden Meaning in Fairytales" by Margret Meyerkort (Adult)
> This article is included in *Lifeways: Working with Family Questions* compiled by Gundrun Davy and Bons Voors. (Stroud, UK: Hawthorn Press, 1983)

Knots On a Counting Rope by Bill Martin, Jr. and John Archambault, Ill. by Ted Rand
> A Native American boy asks his grandfather to recite the story of the boy's life once again. The two weave a tale of love, courage, and strength. (NY: Henry, Holt & Co., 1987)

Laura Charlotte by Kathryn O. Galbraith, Illustrated by Floyd Cooper
> Laura Charlotte listens once again, as her mother tells her the story of Charlotte, the stuffed elephant her mother received as a child, who is now Laura Charlotte's precious playmate. (NY: Philomel, 1990)

The Story Bible by Pearl S. Buck (Adult)
> A good resource to use when memorizing a Bible story to tell aloud. (NY: Random House, 1971)

The Story Girl by L.M. Montgomery
> From the author of *Anne of Green Gables* comes another great work of fiction about a group of children growing up together in the country, and learning of love, honor, and friendship. (Toronto: Bantam, 1989)

The Uses of Enchantment: The Meaning and Importance of Storytelling by Bruno Bettleheim (Adult)
> A profound account of the value of fairytales for children. (NY: Random House, 1977)

When the Beginning Began: Stories about God, the Creatures, and Us by Julius Lester
> Using Jewish legend and his own translation from the Hebrew of the Book of Genesis, Julius Lester weaves tales of humor and wisdom. (NY: Harcourt Brace & Company, 1999)

Listed by religious/spiritual perspective (alphabetically)

Buddhist

The Cat Who Went to Heaven by Elizabeth Coatworth
A timeless fable of a cat who changes the life of an impoverished Japanese painter. The artist has been commissioned to paint a picture for the village temple. He paints a snail, a swan, a horse -- all the animals that received the Buddha's blessing. When the artist decides to include the cat in the painting, he is chastised severely by the temple priest, but then rewarded by a miracle. (NY: Macmillan, 1990)

The First Snow by Helen Coutant
A story in which a grandchild who recently moved with her family from Vietnam to New England learns about death through the experience of her first snowfall. (NY: Alfred A. Knopf, 1974)

The Mountains of Tibet by Mordicai Gerstein
In a small village, high in the mountains of Tibet, there lives a woodcutter who has always longed to travel, but the man grows old without ever leaving the mountain. When he dies, he is offered a chance to choose another life. (NY: Harper & Row, 1987)

See also: *Buddha* and *Sadako and the Thousand Paper Cranes (Biography)*

Christian

The Best Christmas Pageant Ever by Barbara Robinson (8 and up)
This chapter book is full of laughs, as well as a very tender story of a community learning to accept the Herdman children, known as the worst kids in the history of the world. (On the last page, please consider changing the line referring to Mary's picture as "all pink and white and pure-looking," to "all brown and glowing and pure-looking." The fact that Mary (and Jesus) had dark skin is often misrepresented in the Christian church. (NY: HarperCollins, 1972)

The Christmas Miracle of Jonathan Toomey by Susan Wojciechowski, Ill. by P.J. Lynch
A reclusive woodcutter is befriended by a widow and her son, when they ask him to carve a new nativity set in time for Christmas. The request leads to a miracle. (Cambridge: Candlewick Press, 1995)

Pollyanna by Eleanor H. Porter (8 and up)
Pollyanna Whittier is an orphan who must come to live with her crotchety Aunt Polly. But Pollyanna's optimistic attitude has a positive affect on everyone in her new town, including the minister, who has been preaching from a place of anger for far too long.

The Lion, the Witch, and the Wardrobe by C.S. Lewis (8 & up)
The second book in the delightful Narnia series, in which the Lion, Aslan, is a metaphor for Christ.

The Selfish Giant by Oscar Wilde
A selfish giant forbids the neighborhood children to come into his beautiful garden, and soon finds that his selfishness has caused winter to reign eternally there. Then one day, the children sneak back into his garden, bringing spring with them, and the giant discovers a small boy who will change his life forever. (Natick, MA: Picture Book Studio, 1984)

The Singer, The Song, and *The Finale* trilogy by Calvin Miller (14 & up)
A retelling of Jesus' life. This series has been called "a powerful metaphor of incarnation and redemption." (Downers Grove, IL: InterVarsity Press, 1975)

The Tale of Three Trees by Angela Elwell Hunt, Illustrated by Tim Jonke

An enchanting folktale of three trees who each get the wish of their lifetime, as they each play a role in three well-known miracles. (Colorado Springs: Lion Publishing, 1989)

See also: *The Small Woman* (Biographies), *Prayers from the Ark* (Poetry), *Are You There, God? It's Me, Margaret* (Prayer), *The Story Bible* and *When the Beginning Began* (Storytelling), *But God Remembered* and *In God's Name* (Jewish), *The Give-Away* (Native American)

Jewish

But God Remembered: Stories of Women From Creation to the Promised Land and *In God's Name* by Sandy Eisenberg Sasso

Two great picture books by one of the first female rabbis. *But God Remembered* is an array of stories, told in the tradition of Jewish midrash, about Lilith, Serach, Bityah, and the Daughters of Z. *In God's Name* is a story that takes place after the creation of the world, when everyone is in search of the name for God. (Woodstock, VT: Jewish Lights, 1995/1994)

By the Hanukkah Light by Sheldon Oberman, Illustrated by Neil Waldman

When Grandpa celebrated Hanukkah in Europe, he celebrated in the same way children do today, yet Hanukkah was different. Grandpa's family was forced to observe the holiday in secrecy. This is a beautiful story of joy, courage, and healing. (Honesdale, PA: Boyds Mills Press, 1997)

The Family Treasury of Jewish Holidays by Malka Drucker (Adult)

Games, recipes, and songs to celebrate the Jewish holidays. (Boston: Little, Brown, 1994)

Milk and Honey: A Year of Jewish Holidays by Jane Yolen (Adult)

A creative resource for enlivening Jewish celebrations. (NY: G.P. Putnam's Sons, 1996)

Riches by Esther Hautzig

An old couple who have come to retirement age, wonder what their hard-working hands can do to please God. (NY: HarperCollins, 1992)

The Tie Man's Miracle: A Chanukah Tale by Steven Schnur, Illustrated by Stephen Johnson

An old tie salesman comes to a home to peddle his ties, and finds the family ready to celebrate the final evening of Chanukah. The old man has no family to go home to, for he lost his family in the war. In addition to this story of great sorrow, the old man shares the story of a Chanukah miracle, which makes the night unforgettable. (NY: William Morrow & Co., 1995)

A Time for Angels by Karen Hesse (11 & up)

The story of a Jewish girl, separated from her parents by World War I, who survives the flu epidemic of 1918 with the help of an old man and the guidance of an angel. (NY: Hyperion, 1995)

See also: *Anne Frank: The Diary of a Young Girl*, (Biographies), *The Always Prayer Shawl* (Prayer), *When the Beginning Began* (Storytelling)

Multi-Faith

Celebrations of Light by Nancy Luenn

From the Brazilian New Year celebration to the African-American holiday of Kwanzaa, this book circles the year and the globe, showing how light is at the center of our worship, our celebration, our lives. (NY: Atheneum, 1998)

Earth, Water, Fire, Air by Mary Hoffman and Jane Ray
> Myth, legend, images, and ideas from around the world, celebrating the four elements. (Boston: Little, Brown, and Co., 1993)

Illusions: The Adventures of a Reluctant Messiah by Richard Bach (14 & up)
> A modern-day messiah story, that came out of Bach's musings, ". . .what if somebody came along. . . who could teach me how my world works and how to control it? What if I could meet someone super-advanced. What if a Siddhartha or a Jesus came into our time, with power over the illusions of the world because he knew the reality behind them?" This is a mind-stretching novel to consider with a teenager or young adult. Whether you resonant with Bach's story or not, this book is a tremendous conversation starter for considering our own spiritual beliefs. (NY: Delacorte Press, 1977)

Kwanzaa: A Family Affair by Mildred Pitts Walter (Adult)
> One of the most clear, creative, and well-written books on the African-American celebration of Kwanzaa. (NY: Lee & Shepard, 1995)

Old Turtle by Douglas Wood, Illustrated by Cheng-Khee Chee
> This is one of my all-time favorite children's books. It is a fable for children and adults which promotes universal peace and understanding. The animals are arguing about who God is, and Old Turtle intercedes to enlighten them. (Duluth, MN: Pfeifer-Hamilton Publishers, 1992)

The Prophet by Kahlil Gibran (14 & up)
> This classic of poetic prose is imbued with spiritual insight. The story of a prophet, who longs to return to the Isle of his birth. Before his long-awaited ship departs, the people ask him to reveal to them his wisdom of such mysteries as love, joy and sorrow, friendship, religion, death. . . (NY: Alfred A. Knopf, 1923)

See also: *The Little Match Girl* (Fairytales & Folktales), *Grandpa's Garden* and *How Far to Heaven* (Grandparent and Grandchild), *Earth Prayers* and *Life Prayers* (Prayer)

Muslim

Ramadan by Suhaib Hamid Ghazi
> Hakeem and his family anticipate the arrival of the new moon that will signal the beginning of the Islamic celebration of Ramadan. During this holy time, Hakeem observes the rituals of fasting, feasting, sharing, and prayer. (Holiday House, 1996)

Native American

The Give-Away by Ray Buckley
> The animals, seeing that humanity has lost its way, decide to have a "give-away," so each can give a gift that will help humans find their way again. In the end, the Creator tells the animals that the Great Mystery is the One who must do the giving. (Nashville: Abingdon Press, 1999)

The Indian Way: Learning to Communicate with Mother Earth by Gary McLain
> A book of stories and activities which focus on the eve of each full moon, when Grandpa Iron (a Northern Arapahoe medicine man) gathers his grandchildren to tell them stories of wisdom about the earth, plants, animals, our homes, and more. (Santa Fe: John Muir Publications, 1990)

Keepers of Life, Keepers of the Earth, & Keepers of the Animals by Caduto & Bruchac
> Three collections of tales and activities focusing on creation. The authors utilize creative arts, math, sensory awareness, social studies, and writing to foster environmental awareness and responsibility. (Golden, CO: Fulcrum, Inc., 1994/1988/1991)

See also: *Annie and the Old One* (Healing), *Coyote and the Magic Words* and *Knots On a Counting Rope* (Storytelling)

Association of Waldorf Schools of North America
3750 Bannister Road
Fair Oaks, CA   95628
916-961-0927 web site: www.awsna.org

Waldorf education is the fastest-growing education movement today, and serves as a significant resource for public and private school teachers, as well as parents who choose to homeschool. Waldorf education nurtures a child physically, socially, and intellectually, and also recognizes a child's need for *soulful* nourishment in the context of a multi-faith setting. Ongoing training, summer classes and weekend conferences are available for public and private school teachers, and homeschooling parents.

National Association of At-Home Mothers
406 East Buchanan Avenue
Fairfield, IA   52556
e-mail: memberservices@AtHomeMothers.com
web site: www.AtHomeMothers.com

An organization supporting mothers who are at home with children, and those who would like to be. Valuable information and resources for running a home business to help support the decision for at-home parenting.

Parenting for Peace and Justice Network
c/o The Institute for Peace and Justice
4144 Lindell Blvd. #408
St. Louis, MO   63108
314-533-4445 e-mail: PPJN@aol.com

An international interfaith network for parents who wish to work toward a healthy family life in which social ministry is a priority. Co-founder, Jim McGinnis, recently wrote *A Call To Peace: 52 Meditations on the Family Pledge of Nonviolence.*

Musical Instruments

Harps of Lorien
PO Box 77
Questa, NM   97556
505-586-1712 Toll-free: 877-273-8009
web site: www.taosnet.com/harpsoflorien
email: raphael@kitcarson.net

Song of the Sea
47 West Street
Bar Harbor, ME   04609
207-288-5653
web site: www.songsea.com

Workshops

Shea Darian offers the following workshops for parents, grandparents, teachers, and caregivers:

Sanctuaries of Childhood:
Nurturing a Child's Spiritual Life

In a fast-paced, electronic age, how can we as parents and caregivers, provide a curative environment for children in which they may cultivate the capacity for genuine spiritual devotion? Where can children find sanctuaries for soulful nourishment in our world today? As we explore these questions, participants will find inspiration and gain practical tools for serving as a child's spiritual guide.

Seven Times the Sun:
Guiding Your Child Through the Rhythms of the Day

Establishing creative daily patterns and celebrating ordinary moments with children allows parents to avoid many discipline problems, and serves to lift our daily lives into the realm of the sacred. Through presentation, songs, verses, and simple rituals, participants explore how creating daily rhythms and simple celebrations can provide comfort, joy, and balance in a family's life.

Passages of Childhood:
Celebrating Your Child's Life From Birth to the Teenage Years

We live in a society that lacks meaningful celebrations to honor a child's significant developmental passages. Yet, there are many opportunities, as a child's life unfolds, to honor these passages: birth, weaning, the first day of school, penetrating the magic of Santa Claus and the tooth fairy, the "nine-year change," and the changes of puberty. Participants consider how to create celebrations that gift a child with meaningful images to carry with them as they grow.

Music to Melt the Stars:
The Art of Singing With Children

An exploration of the gifts of singing with children. Participants learn a myriad of songs to sing with children throughout the day — including many from Shea's books, *Seven Times the Sun* and *Sanctuaries of Childhood*. Inexperienced and bashful singers, as well as experienced vocalists, will enjoy this exploration of how our singing can bring peace, healing and a deeper sense of community.

Shea Darian also teaches workshops for faith communities in the arts of drama and dance, with an interest in reclaiming these arts as meaningful forms of worship.

Index of Poems, Blessings, and Songs

Also available from Gilead Press. . .

Seven Times the Sun: Guiding Your Child Through the Rhythms of the Day By Shea Darian

A ground-breaking book, cherished by many parents and teachers. *Seven Times the Sun* is full of ideas, reflections, songs, stories, family rituals, and verses that bring balance and celebration to such simple daily events as mealtimes, bedtimes, chores, and play. A practical, creative, and inspiring resource for parenting in the twenty-first century! ($15.95 US)

Celtic Quest CD ~ Avalon a cappella

Enjoy the pure, crystal harmony of this a cappella women's trio, singing original and traditional celtic music. This CD includes original songs by Shea Darian, including "I Married Me an Irish Man," "Water's Edge," and "Set the Spirit Free." Discover why so many have described the music of Avalon a cappella as "deeply moving, a soulful experience." ($14.95 US)

Grandpa's Garden By Shea Darian

A children's picture book, in which grandpa and grandchild work side-by-side in Grandpa's garden, learning firsthand of life, death, growth, and change. A beautiful addition to any child's or grandparent's library!
($7.95 US – paperback, $16.95 US – hardcover)

To order, call or fax Gilead Press (608) 655-1023
or e-mail: gilead@jvlnet.com

Also see the Quick Order Forms on the following pages

Gilead Press Quick Order Form

Telephone orders: (608) 655-1023

Fax orders: (608) 655-1023

E-mail orders: gilead@jvlnet.com

Postal orders: Fill out the form below and mail with check to:
Gilead Press, PO Box 727, Marshall, WI, 53559

Name: _____

Address: _____

City: _____ State: _____ Zip: _____

Telephone: _____

e-mail address: _____

	Quantity	Retail Price	Total
Sanctuaries of Childhood: Nurturing a Child's Spiritual Life		$16.95 US	
Seven Times the Sun: Guiding Your Child Through the Rhythms of the Day		$15.95 US	
Celtic Quest CD – Avalon a cappella		$14.95 US	
Grandpa's Garden – paperback		$7.95 US	
Grandpa's Garden – hardcover		$16.95 US	
Wisconsin Residents 5.5% tax			
Shipping: US $4.00 1st item, $1.00 each additional item.	Shipping		
☐ Please send additional information on workshops.	TOTAL		

Gilead Press PO Box 727 Marshall, WI 53559

Gilead Press Quick Order Form

Telephone orders: (608) 655-1023

Fax orders: (608) 655-1023

E-mail orders: gilead@jvlnet.com

Postal orders: Fill out the form below and mail with check to:
Gilead Press, PO Box 727, Marshall, WI, 53559

Name: _____

Address: _____

City: _____ State: _____ Zip: _____

Telephone: _____

e-mail address: _____

	Quantity	Retail Price	Total
Sanctuaries of Childhood: Nurturing a Child's Spiritual Life		$16.95 US	
Seven Times the Sun: Guiding Your Child Through the Rhythms of the Day		$15.95 US	
Celtic Quest CD – Avalon a cappella		$14.95 US	
Grandpa's Garden – paperback		$7.95 US	
Grandpa's Garden – hardcover		$16.95 US	

Wisconsin Residents 5.5% tax

Shipping: US $4.00 1st item, $1.00 each additional item.   Shipping

☐ Please send additional information on workshops.   TOTAL

Gilead Press PO Box 727 Marshall, WI 53559